DEVIL'S LAKE

Wisconsin

AND THE

CIVILIAN CONSERVATION CORPS

DEVIL'S LAKE

Wisconsin

AND THE

CIVILIAN CONSERVATION CORPS

Robert J. Moore

Charleston — London

THE
History
PRESS

Published by The History Press
Charleston, SC 29403
www.historypress.net

Front cover: Color photo of Devil's Lake courtesy of Robert J. Moore.
Back cover: Color photo of two boys with shovels courtesy of Richard McDavitt.

First published 2011

Manufactured in the United States

ISBN 978.1.60949.277.9

Library of Congress Cataloging-in-Publication Data

Moore, Robert, 1949-
Devil's Lake, Wisconsin, and the Civilian Conservation Corps / Robert Moore.
p. cm.
Includes bibliographical references and index.
ISBN 978-1-60949-277-9
1. Devil's Lake State Park (Wis.)--History. 2. Civilian Conservation Corps (U.S.)--
Wisconsin--Devil's Lake Region--History. I. Title.
F587.S2M66 2011
977.5'76--dc22
2011010588

Notice: The information in this book is true and complete to the best of our knowledge. It is offered without guarantee on the part of the author or The History Press. The author and The History Press disclaim all liability in connection with the use of this book.

This book is dedicated to more than one thousand young enrollees who served in the Civilian Conservation Corps at Devil's Lake, Wisconsin. Along with project supervisors and camp administrators, they changed forever the level of visitors' experiences at Wisconsin's most popular state park.

Contents

Acknowledgements   9

Introduction   11

1. Relief from Hard Times   21
2. The CCC Arrives at the Park   33
3. Daily Life at the Camp   48
4. Baraboo and the Boys   61
5. David Rouse and the Early Years   73
6. Getting the Job Done   80
7. Art McDavitt's Long Road to Devil's Lake   107
8. The Camp Newspaper   113
9. Farewell   125

Notes   143
Bibliography   151
Index   155
About the Author   159

Acknowledgements

Finding and pulling together the pieces of history that are needed to tell a good story is for me the most enjoyable part of writing a book. The most compelling part of the Civilian Conservation Corps' (CCC) story is finding the old veterans who served in the camps. Another is the photographic evidence they left behind.

The most numerous collection of pictures is found among the archives at Devil's Lake State Park. Having access to the park archives was the most important element in telling the story of the CCC boys at the lake. Naturalist Dave Bouche at Devil's Lake State Park, Wisconsin, was the single most important research aid. He generously opened the historical records of the park and was also helpful in locating buildings and hidden CCC work in the park. His hospitality made my visits to the park one of the best experiences of this project.

The National Association of Civilian Conservation Corps Alumni (NACCCA), since reconstituted as the Civilian Conservation Corps Legacy, was also helpful. Archivist Harry Dallas and Donna Broome were most helpful in pointing my research in the right direction.

The text records of the CCC camp at Devil's Lake came mostly from the National Archives Branch in College Park, Maryland. I have archivist Gene Morris to thank for guiding me through the maze of government documents and answering my questions about the bureaucracy of the CCC.

The staff at the Sauk County Historical Society Museum in Baraboo, Wisconsin, was very helpful in providing access to its CCC collection of newspaper clippings.

Providing historical background information was Kenneth Lange of Baraboo. His books, plus our conversations about Devil's Lake, were a great starting point.

Carol Alhgren of Minneapolis was a great source for understanding the architectural reasoning behind the park buildings.

More than anything else, this investigation would have never begun without a suggestion from my wife, Lois. Time after time, she urged me to take the highway turnoff to Devil's Lake. She had been there before, and I hadn't. I resisted, thinking it was probably just like all the other lakes in Wisconsin. I was wrong. And that first visit (in winter) sparked an interest that has not subsided.

Special thanks go to the families of CCC veterans who shared stories and photographs. Especially instrumental was Richard McDavitt, whose trove of snapshots collected by his father added new elements and evidence to the historical record. Wilma Stone Crow and Betty Krueger also shared stories that could be found nowhere else.

The final tribute goes to the veterans of the CCC at Devil's Lake. I found so few of them, but their remembrances spurred me on to tell as much as I could about their historic contributions. Emil Pradarelli, Louie Roedell and Robert Spees provided perspective from other camp locations. Walter Lahl, Bruce Budde, Clarence Guetzkow and Ted Rozinski served full tours at the lake. They, along with their families, were so very generous and cooperative in sharing as much information as they could remember.

INTRODUCTION

Only teenagers on a dare would try a stunt like this. It was a climb of five hundred feet to the top of the bluff over slick and icy chunks of rock. Many of the boulders were as big as an automobile. Most of the climb was open and exposed to the elements. Yet the boys were not afraid. They knew the dangers that lay ahead of them. They had climbed the East Bluff of Devil's Lake many times before, but it was different this time. This time, they faced winter conditions on the jagged rocks. There would be patches of ice, and the exposed boulders would quickly numb fingers that were not protected with gloves. All of that didn't matter to the small group of young men looking up at the bluff. This was not a work assignment, and it was not a rescue mission. This time, it was just for fun.

It was not a technical climb and did not require any sophisticated equipment, but it was a dangerous attempt nonetheless. If they wanted to be safe, they would have to take it slow. But that probably wasn't going to happen. The impatience of youth gripped them all. They hurried through their preparations. Instead of climbing ropes and other mountaineering gear, the group simply put on warm clothes, and each member carried a pack containing water and a sack lunch. One of them had a camera.

Winter was the off-season at Devil's Lake, so they didn't see anyone else as they started the climb. No one would be watching from below. They knew friends would be waiting after they came down and would be willing to help them if things went bad, but it would take a couple of hours or more to get a seriously injured climber off the bluff and to a hospital. The greatest danger was that most of the hike had to be negotiated over a steeply pitched talus

A rare winter view of the Devil's Lake CCC camp taken from the top of the East Bluff, circa 1937. *Courtesy Wisconsin Department of Natural Resources (DNR), Devil's Lake State Park.*

slope of icy boulders and loose rock. To the invincible young men on the way up, all the hazards and risks that briefly crossed their minds hardly mattered. The first part of the hike through the trees was easy. They continued up at a steady pace but had to stop occasionally. Even for healthy young men, drawing deep breaths in this cold hurt their chests. As they moved out of the trees and onto the exposed talus slope, the wind became stronger and the footing more slippery. Finally, the white pines near the summit gave them some cover. Then, suddenly, they were on top of the plateau.

They had seen the view from the top of East Bluff many times, mostly in the green splendor of summer, with boats on the lake and bathers in miniature wading in the shallow south beach far below. Looking down on the south side that day, they saw a winter wonderland of snow. The park had a quiet and lonely feeling, but that's why they came on this day. Down below, about a quarter mile east of the lakeshore, was a set of buildings lined up in rows. Even from the top of the bluff, the building complex looked impressive. If the boys didn't know better, they would think it was a school. What they were looking at instead was the Civilian Conservation Corps (CCC) camp built in 1935, still looking bright and new.

One of the most important pieces of equipment on this climbing trip was the camera. A number of boys had made this trip and taken a photo of the camp, but this picture was going to be a winter view. Not many boys would have a picture like that, only ones who were brave enough to climb the East Bluff on a bitter winter's day. The picture was going to be sent to the folks back home to show them where they had spent the last year. Hopefully, it would end up in the family scrapbook alongside the pictures of their high school graduations. Since it was such a special view, an extra copy might be made and given to the camp commander. It might look good in the office. It was a unique view at a unique time, but then, everything about Devil's Lake was unique. The young CCC boys atop the East Bluff at Devil's Lake had good reason to believe that their camp assignment was the best. Their obviously biased evaluation was not unfounded. It was not only the job but also the location. In the fledgling Wisconsin state park system, some areas were more equal (and accessible) than others. In a grouping of equals, Devil's Lake seemed to be even more equal than others. Its increased status had everything to do with its location, transportation links, and the related upswing each year in tourist visitation.[1]

In the late nineteenth century, railroads were the key to prosperity. Lumber in the far north and dairy everywhere else propelled the growth of railroads in Wisconsin. Railroad barons were attracted to new locations by the potential for making money on freight, not people. Devil's Lake and surrounding Sauk County had neither an abundance of wood (at least not enough to make railroading profitable) nor a significant dairy operation. What the area did have was a tourist gem that was growing in popularity. That popularity was the key to attracting a railroad to Sauk County.

The lake eventually got its rail connection, but it was a mixed blessing.

Tomahawk Rock and the north beach, circa 1918. Note the double railroad tracks hugging the eastern shore. *Courtesy Robert J. Moore.*

13

However, in the 1870s, few people saw the coming of the railroad as a mixed blessing. It would take almost a century for a groundswell of environmental awareness to point out that a ribbon of rails in the park was not consistent with the natural characteristics of the area. In the meantime, none of that mattered. What mattered was development and progress, and a railroad was the first step. The second step was to provide people a place to stay. If tourism at Devil's Lake was to be successful, it was obvious to civic leaders and businessmen of towns near the lake that accommodations were needed to meet the demands of long-distance visitors. Development plans were grand and in some cases luxuriant, thanks in large part to the reliability of the railroad. Magnificent resort hotels were built, and comfortable excursion boats cruised the lake. It was the Gilded Age in America, and at the same time it was the "Golden Age of Luxury" at Devil's Lake. Rail transportation made it all possible.[2]

Alas, the prosperity of the Gilded Age did not last. But even after the resort hotels were gone, railroads were still a popular transportation option

Cliff House during the 1890s. This was the most luxurious hotel at Devil's Lake during the heyday of the resort period. Room rates were $2.50 per day, with the railroad depositing visitors within a few feet of the hotel entrance. Poor management decisions and squabbles with the railroad doomed the resort, and it was closed in 1904. The hotel was torn down shortly thereafter. *Courtesy Wisconsin DNR, Devil's Lake State Park.*

into the park. But that would change, too. By the time the first group of Civilian Conservation Corps boys arrived at Devil's Lake in 1934, the automobile had taken over as the most convenient way to visit the lake. The independence that came with the car had an impact on the park, much like the railroads had eighty years before. Attendance exploded.

Since the 1950s, Devil's Lake has consistently been the most visited park in the Wisconsin system. A significant part of that appeal is due to its popularity beyond central Wisconsin. Geography was always a friend to Devil's Lake. Chicago, Milwaukee, Madison and even Minneapolis were all within manageable travel distance of the lake. One of the biggest draws to the lake came from Chicago, less than two hundred miles to the southeast. From the railroad days of the late nineteenth century to the resort hotel period around the turn of the twentieth century and beyond, residents of the Windy City have perpetuated a long-standing love affair with Devil's Lake—this from a population that has one of the mighty Great Lakes on its doorstep.

Tired urbanites have always found respite by Devil's Lake. Word-of-mouth was enough, and one example is representative of how a good thing traveled on the lips of city folks. Lois Krzeminski and her high school friends from the ethnic Cragin neighborhood of northwest Chicago had many recreational opportunities to choose from in the city. One of their favorites was the North Avenue beach on Lake Michigan. The good news for them was that it wasn't far from home. The bad news was that it was downtown, with all the traffic and noise. Riding on a crowded city bus in one's swimsuit was not the kind of atmosphere that Lois and her friends thought about when they imagined getting away from it all. There had to be an alternative—something more natural and less urban. Word spread through her circle of city friends. There was a place. It was a bit of a drive compared to North Avenue, someone said, but it would be worth it.

Looking back on it all, Lois's best memories of walking on the beach on a hot summer's day are not from those in the shadows of Windy City skyscrapers but from her 1970s camping days at Devil's Lake. While there, she had seen the stone buildings at the Wisconsin park but didn't know about the CCC work back then; she just knew it was a great place to camp, swim, rent a boat, buy an ice cream and experience the natural beauty of the lake. Hordes of tourists had come before her, and millions more would follow her each year.[3]

Seventy years before Lois's first visit, Devil's Lake businessmen were bragging about their connection to Chicago's elite families, like the Revells and Gilletts. A hotel publication at the lake reported that late nineteenth-century politician and popular five-time mayor of Chicago Carter Harrison had considered Devil's Lake to be his favorite summer resort. That was during the heyday of the hotel resort period.[4] In 1935, the CCC would find the amenities at the lake far different from when Harrison and his entourage lounged by the shore in the 1880s. Some would say things had gone downhill since Harrison's day. The lakeside resorts were gone. Even the remaining camping amenities looked worn out and haphazard by the 1920s. The park needed a facelift. That was why the CCC boys came to Devil's Lake.

Thousands of teenagers and young adults embarked on the adventure of a lifetime when they joined the Civilian Conservation Corp during the Great Depression years of the 1930s. Even though many saw it as an adventure, the program was not intended as a recreational or vacation experience. It was a program of outdoor work, and everyone who went in knew that. They also knew that the CCC was part of a massive relief program to help people get through the tough economic times. But beyond the work, the CCC opportunity was a chance to get away from familiar surroundings and experience the world outside their hometowns. Some had spent their young lifetimes growing up within a few miles of where they were born. Many felt they had something to prove, and the CCC gave them that chance. Beyond the adventure, perhaps more than anything, it was a way they could show their folks how mature, productive and independent they could be.

The confidence, fun and a sense of independence can be seen on the faces of the young men in this CCC work crew at Devil's Lake in 1937. *Courtesy Richard McDavitt.*

This book is intended to focus on the CCC camp at Devil's Lake. Doing so will show why the CCC was the most successful of the New Deal relief programs. The stories of the young men bring out the adventure, fear, loneliness, friendship and cooperative spirit that made these men part of the "greatest generation" of Americans. The stories will also show that the CCC experience carried over beyond the Depression years to have an impact on the national character as America entered World War II. The stories will take the reader back to a time in which leaving home and accepting responsibility was the key to economic survival, as well as the path to personal maturity in an era of crushing economic despair.

The level of desperation was unprecedented, and every household felt its effects. Leaders in Washington seemed paralyzed. The economic crash that began in the fall of 1929 had become a crisis the American government did not know how to handle. As the economy spiraled down, the American public had a chance to speak—at the ballot box. The presidential election of 1932 brought a new administration that heard the message on election day. Franklin D. Roosevelt came to Washington determined to offer a "New Deal" and try new things.

Among the first laws to pass was one directed at helping young people. A central component of that law was the creation of the Civilian Conservation Corps. It was one of Roosevelt's favorite projects and one that not only would provide relief for young men but was also an opportunity to restore and improve the nation's forests, farms and parks. To the young men who joined, it was a chance to embark on a grand adventure while working and making a little money. The program was a rousing success.

On one level, it was an environmental success that changed America's perception about conservation. But the true legacy of the Civilian Conservation Corps is found within the young men themselves. In the depths of the Depression, the CCC gave young men something that carried them through the bad times but also laid the foundation for future success. That new element in their lives was hope. The CCC was a realization that somebody cared about them and was willing to give them a chance. That chance included development of skills on the job that could be used to make a better life.

The stories of work and play the young men brought back after their service at Devil's Lake were noteworthy in at least two ways. First, while their adventures away from home were unique and special to each individual, the stories were tied together with tens of thousands of others who enrolled elsewhere in the United States. They all had something in common, even though they served in camps hundreds and even thousands of miles apart. Ironically, most of the stories are not about the actual work that was done on the land. Mostly, they are stories of friendships and survival skills. For example, Emil Pradarelli was a young CCC boy who served in a camp in the north woods of Wisconsin. When asked decades later what he got out of his service, he didn't mention trail building or brush clearing. He simply said, "I picked up some important knowledge on getting along with other people."[5]

Second, the variety of their work assignments, learning experiences and time away from home taught them life lessons about responsibility, pride in one's work and teamwork on the job. Such revelations happened all across America, no matter where the boys served. Oftentimes, the men didn't realize they were learning those lessons until they got home. Time and again, the veterans say that their CCC training got them ready for military life and gave them the maturity and moral character to face down fascism in World War II.

The story of the CCC and the young men who did the work is also a story of local geography and how the land was changed. Therefore, this book seeks to show how the landscape had an impact on the men and the kind of work that engaged them. Conservation was the middle name of the organization, and the kind of projects the boys were asked to complete depended on the condition of the land. But the CCC boys were not policymakers and therefore not decision makers. The young men didn't get a chance to say what kind of projects were good for a particular area. It was understandable and correct that the CCC boys didn't have that kind of input. They had no training and no experience in forest management, soil conservation or park development. Few of the CCC boys or even their job foremen were true naturalists or conservationists. There were government officials and other people directing the work who had a naturalist's sense of purpose and environmental sensitivity. That is why the CCC story at Devil's Lake and elsewhere is special; the CCC stories of work are stories of survival, adventure and fun.

The CCC work that was done in the state park system mirrors the kind of work that was done at the big national parks out West. By looking at the state park work in Wisconsin, it is possible to see how CCC administrators, who at first gave special attention to the "crown jewel" national parks of the West, later used the expertise of the National Park Service to improve existing state parks and move the national conservation focus beyond tree planting and trail building in the West.

The adventure part of being in the CCC started not when a young man signed the paper to join but when he received his camp assignment. In the Midwest, there were dozens of camp assignments that could have come his way—some significantly more desirable than others. Under the CCC organizational umbrella, there were many agencies to which a young man could be assigned for conservation work. For example, he could be assigned to a camp that did jobs for the Federal Reclamation Project or the Department of Grazing. In an era of tough times, it is probably true that most young men did not care where their CCC work took them. Yet as the CCC program developed in the upper Midwest, the overwhelming number of assignments for the new recruits focused on supervision by one of three government agencies. They were the U.S. Forest Service, which had jurisdiction over the national forest lands; the National Park Service, which also would assist state parks; and the Soil Conservation Service, which supervised work on farmland.

Of all the agencies supervising CCC work, perhaps the most visible to the general public was the National Park Service (NPS). The park service is part of the Department of Interior and is most famously known as the guardian of our natural wonders in the American West. Grand Canyon, Yellowstone and Yosemite, for example, conjure up images of not only waterfalls and magnificent gorges but also friendly rangers guiding tourists and giving campground talks around a cozy, crackling fire. Wisconsin has a few notable gorges but no soaring mountains. Yet the state has natural wonders worth protecting. Wisconsin used its state parks as the hook necessary to attract NPS management and CCC manpower and expand its opportunities for conservation projects in the state.

The CCC was at the forefront of the national conservation effort during the 1930s, but despite its many accomplishments, few people cared to hear about the experiences of the young workers after the program ended in 1942. There was a world war to fight, and afterward folks just wanted to get on with their lives. Memories naturally fade as the years go by. For those

With the south face of the East Bluff in the background, National Park Service job supervisors conduct an outdoor class at camp. Meetings of this kind were common before starting a major trail or construction project. *Courtesy Wisconsin DNR, Devil's Lake State Park.*

CCC veterans who survived into the twenty-first century, there remain bits and pieces of information. They are real but fragmented. It is those bits and pieces that help fill in the CCC history of Wisconsin. Their never-before-heard voices are what can be found in this book.

The CCC men recognized that they were part of a grand American experiment. Mindful of that, many of them had cameras at the ready. They took pictures not only to preserve the personal memories of friendships and adventures but also to remember a historic and adventuresome time that would quickly pass. Many of those who had no camera purchased prints from other recruits. Before they died, some of them left their old black-and-white photographs with the agencies that had employed them. But for most, their snapshots remained in family albums, stored at the bottom of a cedar chest or in a shoebox in the back of a closet. Over the years, some of the photos were inadvertently thrown out and lost forever.

The surviving CCC veterans have their own private memories, but those are fading too, just like the old photographs. Their experiences remain a part of a hidden history, and it is worthwhile to recover as many memories as possible. Their work in Wisconsin is impressive in its scale and impact. But in a larger context, the efforts of the young men mentioned here are typical of the amazing burst of woodland conservation work at the parks, forests and farms of the Midwest and elsewhere across the country during the Depression era. Ordinary Americans outside the CCC who never thought much about preservation and conservation saw and heard what was going on in the 1930s and began to pay attention. It was a slow transition from that awareness to the full-blown environmental campaign that began with the first Earth Day in 1970, but it was a beginning.

The popularity of Devil's Lake makes it the logical choice to more closely examine the CCC effort. Having to select one park among the many beautiful state parks of Wisconsin is difficult. Yet what made the CCC effort at Devil's Lake special was its visibility. Devil's Lake was and is the most popular park destination in Wisconsin. The long history of Devil's Lake, its abundant records and its surviving CCC veterans make it the best and most representative choice to show readers what life was like at a state park camp. Doing that means relating the experiences of those who were there. Unfortunately, most of those Great Depression boys are gone. But the stories of a few can still be told. Bruce Budde, Clarence Guetzkow, Art McDavitt, David Rouse, Walter Lahl and Eugene Odbert all served at Devil's Lake, and their experiences go beyond the official records to help fill out a more complete history of the CCC at the park.

1

RELIEF FROM HARD TIMES

In the fall of 1936, Henry Larson was going back home. However, before he left, he wanted to sum up his experiences in Wisconsin. Henry was not a tourist; nor was he a longtime resident ready for retirement. He was a CCC boy who had been stationed at Devil's Lake State Park. He had been through an incredible adventure, but it had been one that he shared with hundreds of other young men at the lake. He had only a few lines in the camp newspaper in which to explain:

> *After twenty-three months of service…the lessons I have learned are many. I have learned the value of discipline and why it is so necessary. I have learned to cooperate with my fellow workers but at the same time to be independent and stand on my own two feet. [Also] the value of good health and clean living, fair play and good sportsmanship and what it really means.*[6]

It was an unexpected statement of maturity coming from a person barely out of his teens. Unfortunately, Henry did not detail the experiences he had been through. Yet it is possible to understand and tell his story through the mutual adventures of the people he worked with and those who came after him. It's not a complete picture, but it is one that is representative of what went on at dozens of CCC camps in Wisconsin during the Great Depression.

When Henry left the CCC in 1936, the nation was in the midst of the worst economic crisis in its history. In the old days, these troubles were called "panics" and were often short-lived. This time, the bad times were hanging on too long, and worse still, nobody knew when or if the good life would be coming back. The word panic was replace by another term—depression.

The economic health of Wisconsin was more than ever tied to agriculture. To be sure, many farmers got through the economic storm and brought in a harvest each fall without much help from the government. But there was a feeling in the land that if a significant number of farmers were in trouble, then problems were certain to come along sooner or later for everyone else. Such fears were well founded considering that slightly over 21 percent of the American workforce was employed in agriculture in 1930.[7]

As bad as things were on the farm, they were equally as desperate in the cities. National unemployment reached its peak at 25 percent of the workforce in the spring of 1933. It didn't drop below 10 percent until 1942. One-third of those still on the job were working part time. The average wage in a manufacturing job in 1929 was over $24.50 per week. By 1933, it had fallen to $16.65. Automobile production fell by one-third from 1929 to 1932. Other industries related to cars were naturally affected when the auto assembly line slowed. For example, production of iron and steel fell by 60 percent compared to pre-crash days. Production by machine toolmakers went down by almost two-thirds.[8]

Throughout America, the anthem of the times was "Brother, can you spare a dime?" with frustration and occasional desperation as hallmarks of everyday life. Men who had known work throughout their entire adult lives were weighed down by the thought that family members were counting on the man of the house to make things right. It was a heavy burden.

Another kind of burden and frustration in the workforce was found among young men—many just graduated from high school. Concern for them was well founded. With few employable job skills in a shrinking market, their chance of finding work was gone almost before it started. Each day, young teenagers had to compete with adults for even part-time work. It was not surprising that during the Depression, unemployment among young people and those over sixty years of age was significantly higher compared to the regular workforce. Older teenagers began to think about their stations in life. Guilt overcame many young men. They were old enough to help and felt it was their duty to do something to support the family. But they weren't sure what that duty entailed.

They roamed the sidewalks of their hometowns, peering into storefronts. Having recently graduated from high school, or in some cases dropped out of school, they had few prospects. What vocational or trade skills they may have had were often picked up working around the house or farm. It wasn't enough. U.S. representative Thomas Amlie saw it happening around the courthouse square in his southern Wisconsin hometown of Elkhorn: "The young people will gather in the morning, hang around, just sit there until it is time to go home for dinner or for supper, very much the same as the retired farmers have been doing for over eighty years."[9]

When Franklin D. Roosevelt became president in 1933, he was determined to take bold action to turn the economy around by offering the nation a "New Deal." Early in his presidency, Roosevelt talked Congress into creating a number of agencies, all designed to bring relief to a certain segment of the economy. Historians called them an "alphabet soup" because the new agencies were best known through their initials. Among them were the AAA (Agriculture Adjustment Administration), PWA (Public Works Administration) and NRA (National Recovery Administration).[10]

The Emergency Conservation Work (ECW) law was the official title of the new conservation legislation, but everyone came to know it as the

President Franklin D. Roosevelt, seated third from right, and dignitaries visit a CCC camp in the Shenandoah Valley, Virginia, in August 1933. Seated next to the president (wearing the dark necktie) is Robert Fechner, national director of the CCC. Seated next to Fechner is Harold Ickes, secretary of interior, which also has jurisdiction over the National Park Service. *Courtesy Franklin D. Roosevelt Presidential Library, Hyde Park, New York.*

Civilian Conservation Corps. Many people would later say that it was the best-remembered and most successful program of the Great Depression years. Its premise was simple and direct. Roosevelt's idea was to hire and train an army of young men who would work outdoors in the forests, parks and farms of America. The program would not only give hope, training and employment to America's youth, but it would also take a giant stride toward conservation and preservation of the country's natural resources. In the few short weeks following the new president's inauguration, the organizational wheels began to turn, and the CCC opened its doors for business.

Getting the word out and recruiting young men was the first order of business. The rules of eligibility changed slightly as the program evolved during the 1930s, but there were some basic requirements at the beginning. Enrollment in the CCC was open to unemployed, unmarried young men between the ages of eighteen and twenty-five. The men were paid thirty dollars per month, twenty-five dollars of which was sent to parents or relatives back home. Knowing that twenty-five dollars was sent home each month also meant that the young recruit was taking responsibility for family affairs. Devil's Lake enrollee David Rouse was one of thousands who knew the money that was sent home would be put to good use. "My mother made a down payment on a new washing machine with her first twenty-five-dollar check. With six children to care for, she needed it badly."[11] Likewise, Milwaukee-area native Emil Pradarelli understood the importance of joining the CCC to help the family:

> *There was no work for my father in 1937 so the money that was sent home by the CCC was just about the only money coming in for them. They used it to pay household expenses, and believe me, they appreciated every dollar.*[12]

Enrollment in the CCC was for a period of six months, but the young man could reenlist again for a maximum total of one year. Later, terms of enrollment were expanded to allow for six-month reenlistments up to two years total time. Technicalities in the law eventually allowed a few skilled enrollees to stay beyond the two-year limit. For newcomers, the standard practice immediately after signing enrollment papers and taking a physical exam was to head off for fitness training at a military facility and then on to a camp with about two hundred other enrollees (as they were called in official reports) as part of a company unit.[13]

For administrative purposes, the country was divided into "corps" areas. Wisconsin, Illinois and Michigan were grouped together to form the Sixth

Corps. State government agencies worked with the U.S. Department of Labor to develop a type of quota system to determine the number of enrollees needed in each region. The effect of this regional-style organization was to group new recruits in companies with other young men from the same state or geographic corps area. Knowing many of the boys would be away from home for the first time, organizers thought the system would increase camaraderie and local pride by keeping them relatively close to home. But that quickly changed, given the rural nature of conservation projects matched with the urban populations looking for work. Ultimately, there were no guarantees that enrollees would be able to join the CCC and serve in camps near their hometowns.

Young Alfred Krueger was a sickly child who grew up in Baraboo, Wisconsin. He joined the CCC out of a need to help his family, but he also joined to build up his body and improve his fitness. At that time, recruits were given an opportunity to request a particular camp assignment, and administrators generally granted the request when "practicable." If a camp roster were full, for example, it would not be possible to send a new recruit to that camp. Young Alfred apparently signed up at an inconvenient time for officials, for instead of assigning him to the Devil's Lake camp a few short miles down the road, he was sent to the northern woodlands to Camp Sawyer in appropriately named Winter, Wisconsin. Regrettably, Alfred never made it to Devil's Lake as a CCC enrollee. Furthermore, his true feelings about his duty station remained unknown because he purposely never said anything about being passed over for an assignment at his beautiful hometown park.[14]

Each young man had his own reasons for joining the CCC, most of them associated with the need for money plus the desire for personal independence. However, in many cases, there was a special story that guided certain young men toward CCC enrollment. Most of those stories are lost to history, but there are a few that survive and add a special twist to the usual reasons for joining up. One such case was Hiram Calkins, "Hi" to all his friends. In 1939, Calkins was barely getting by as a gravedigger in Poynette, Wisconsin. During his long off-hours, he spent time at the Super ice cream shop in nearby Portage. There he met Helen Peterson, a lovely young high school senior. Their courtship did not go well, and a destructive argument followed. Hi declared he was breaking off the relationship and, in a pique of anger and showmanship, declared to Helen that he was joining the CCC and going far away. Reminiscent of the young lads who left behind broken romances and joined the French Foreign Legion, Hi made good on his promise and signed up. Like the Foreign Legion soldiers of old, Hi believed his experience in a

Wisconsin

Wisconsin and Devil's Lake State Park. *Courtesy Ty Moore.*

new land would make Helen pine for him as time went on. Hi believed his service would make him a more mature and appealing catch. The countless reasons why young men were motivated to sign up for the CCC will never be known, but it seems almost certain that at least a few other young men were drawn to the CCC as a means of dealing with broken hearts. For Hi, his CCC camp assignment was just down the road at Devil's Lake, and he and Helen would happily reunite during his service.[15]

All camps, no matter where they were located, were assigned a coded number for administrative purposes. The designation was based on which agency of government was going to direct the work at each camp. For example, F-34-W at Blackwell denotes a national forest camp (F) whose supervising agency was the U.S. Forest Service. The camp was assigned a number (34) and state letter (W; not always used) denoting the state of

Wisconsin. Camps operating in state parks and supervised by the National Park Service used "SP" followed by the appropriate camp number.

Regardless of name or number, a company of two hundred men was assigned to each camp. Assignments of company numbers also followed a pattern. In a company like #604, the first number signified the Sixth Corps area of the country, with the other numbers simply counting as a sequential number as the units were set up. In companies of four digits, such as 2669, the second number from the left equaled the corps area. With thousands of camps scattered all over the country, the numbering system for both camps and companies was easy to follow for the men and easy to track for CCC administrators. For example, Company 2669 was assigned to camp SP-12. The company number would always remain the same, no matter where the unit was assigned. As for SP-12 the first letters of the camp signified a state park, followed by the park number. In this case, all men of the company knew SP-12 by its geographic name—Devil's Lake.

The U.S. Army had primary control over the young men who enrolled in the program, yet there were important exceptions. While the army operated the camps and had control over where the men would live and eat, nearly all job assignments, work supervision and skills training were handled by the U.S. Forest Service, National Park Service or Soil Conservation Service—otherwise known as the "technical services." Camps would eventually be set up in all states, and various government agencies and technical services would be active in all those states.

It seemed logical and natural that the Forest Service and National Park Service would be first in line to request and supervise work from the CCC. The nature of their mission of conservation and preservation was a perfect fit for the kind of work the young men would be doing as part of the new relief agency. Indeed, the Forest Service and National Park Service had a bureaucracy already in place to process and begin jobs immediately. The National Park Service wasted no time in presenting its requests for CCC work at the national parks and monuments throughout the United States. The big advantage for the NPS was that it already had a general master plan that outlined development requirements in the parks. Now, with new manpower available, National Park director Horace Albright instructed individual park officials to quickly come up with their own specific lists of work projects for their specific locations. Those early requests focused on projects at the big parks out West, like Grand Teton, Glacier, Yosemite and Grand Canyon.[16]

It was assumed that state park officials would work with NPS officials to get CCC workers, but since everything was new, there was confusion about how that would actually happen. The legal authority to include state and municipal parks in planning was solidly in place, but exactly how those parks could benefit, and more importantly, who would control the projects and purse strings relating to CCC work, was uncharted territory to NPS administrators. Unlike the Forest Service, the National Park Service had little experience in sharing information and coordinating preservation and conservation efforts with state park officials.

Complicating matters was the fact that most states did not have a long-standing (or any), formal state park program. Even if they did, many did not have proper planning standards that would have work projects in the park integrate into a master plan for development. In response, the NPS created a completely new department, the Branch of Planning and State Cooperation, later renamed the State Park Division of the ECW, to officially bring the state parks into the NPS planning and work program so they could take advantage of CCC labor. The move to create a new planning department to accelerate work programs at the state parks was necessary and noble, but of course it made no difference to states without parks systems of their own.

A plus for Wisconsin was that it not only had a state parks system, but it also had a system based on the recommendations of one of the top landscape architects in the United States. John Nolen would make his career reputation in the field of urban planning and design at several cities throughout the country, contributing greatly to the look of Madison, the capital city. While Nolen's 1909 formal recommendations and subsequent state park system start-up plan were not extensive, they were still ahead of their time when compared to the efforts of other states. He urged action in large part because he had seen what had happened in many of those other states: "Is Wisconsin going to follow the example of the more populous eastern states and wait until action is difficult, if not impossible, or is it going to learn from their mistakes?" Nolen was wise to recommend standards and action for Wisconsin while there was still time to save some natural areas. He said, "While the state…is large, the amount of natural scenery suited in character, location, and extent for public parks is relatively limited and the best is apt to be taken first by private individuals."[17]

Leading the citizen charge in favor of creating a state park at Devil's Lake was Baraboo businessman William H. McFetridge. He made a compelling case in the self-published pamphlet *An Appeal for the Preservation of the Devil's Lake Region*. The pamphlet gained a wide audience of influential people because it did not come across as a dry government report. Nor was it filled with emotionally charged rhetoric. It was a straightforward, well-written

Camping at the park in the 1920s. The prosperity of the Roaring Twenties, plus the popularity of travel to the park by car, threatened to overwhelm already overcrowded campground facilities. *Courtesy Robert J. Moore.*

defense of park status not only for the lake but also for the surrounding territory, complete with photographs. In 1911, Devil's Lake became one of the first parks of the new Wisconsin system.[18]

It would have seemed logical that with state park status, Devil's Lake and other state parks would have little difficulty getting CCC work. However, issues over supervision of work projects that had arisen elsewhere in the country at the state and local government levels now came up in Wisconsin. For example, there were some state officials who were not sure about bureaucrats from Washington telling Wisconsin what was best for them. C.L. Harrington was the superintendent for Wisconsin state parks and forests from 1923 to 1958. In 1934, he remarked, "I don't like this taking money from Washington because then Washington can dictate to you what you can do and what you can't do. But the pressure's building up on me and I guess I've got to give in."[19] Harrington did indeed give in, but he expressed his continued misgivings about Washington's interference in state projects long after the CCC program was over.

When state parks were added to the CCC jobs list, it was natural that the NPS would take the lead in administering those projects. The NPS had experience in park construction; plus, its guidance over all state park projects would add a degree of uniformity—in building designs, for example—to the kinds of work that would be done. Even after accepting NPS jurisdiction over state park work, Wisconsin and other states did not abdicate their

Built by CCC boys inside the Northern Lights campground loop, this structure is one of the best examples of the rustic architectural style preferred by the National Park Service. *Courtesy Wisconsin DNR, Devil's Lake State Park.*

interests in promoting and requesting specific projects that used CCC labor. But NPS and CCC controlled federal funds to pay for projects. It sounds very confusing, but construction of the buildings at Devil's Lake by the CCC under the guidance of an NPS master plan serves as a good example of what everyone, including Wisconsin officials, wanted for their parks.

A master plan for the park was prepared by the Wisconsin State Park Authority and was reviewed and approved by the NPS regional office in Omaha. Uniformity in style and construction of buildings at Devil's Lake was based on an NPS plan that insisted on design guidelines using what was known as the "rustic" architectural style. In its simplest form, the NPS guidelines "emphasized that park buildings should be as unobtrusive as possible," using native materials that blended the building with the surrounding area. Later guidelines characterized the look of the buildings as giving "the feeling of having been executed by pioneer craftsman with limited hand tools." The NPS already had a lot of experience in this type of architectural landscape design. By 1935, the National Park Service had been through a decade and a half of accelerated building projects at the big parks out West, using the rustic architectural style.

In late 1935, the NPS published a volume, funded in part by the CCC, of structural standards for all kinds of park work. The expanded 1938 version, called simply *Parks and Recreation Structures*, was a three-volume how-to guide that included various photographic examples of native-material construction from throughout the state and national parks of America. It became the bible for planners and landscape architects who had anything to do with park construction. Besides showing pictures of park buildings like visitors' centers, museum buildings and pay stations, the book included photographs of things like incinerators, trail steps, culverts, campfire circles and even park service gates—all designed to make the amenities more rustic and rugged. The publication's text gave voice to the architectural style:

> *Park structures exist for the sole use of the public, it is not required that it be seen from some distance…the park structure is designed with a view to subordinate it to its environment, and is located so that it may profit from any natural screening that may exist.*[20]

While John Nolen, in his 1909 report, praised Devil's Lake as a park site, he also noted the "ravages of the railroad, the quarries, and the scars of commonplace cottages" at the lake. While the CCC was not asked to correct those problems, they were asked, by virtue of the NPS plan, to focus construction in the park on one design concept that would create uniformity, use native materials and thus visually fit with the other natural features of

The bathhouse on the north side of the lake exhibits the intention of planners to use native stone and timber to blend with the shoreline and trees. This 1936 photo shows the east dressing court enclosed with cedar logs. *Courtesy Wisconsin DNR, Devil's Lake State Park.*

the park. Such attention to natural design, landscaping and minimal impact on the land would especially manifest itself in the native stone buildings put up in the park during the CCC years.

Once the authorization had been given for the state parks and NPS planning partnership, the bureaucratic wheels turned swiftly. The CCC district office in Fort Sheridan, Illinois, became responsible for choosing a camp location and getting a company of enrollees to the parks in order to begin work. It also began making arrangements to contract for, and ship, food and building supplies to the new camp. Similar arrangements were being made for all parks on the list, but unlike some of the other state parks in Wisconsin, CCC officials at the district level already knew about Devil's Lake and the kinds of projects that needed to be done. Strictly speaking, they had been there before.

It was common for the CCC, once a main camp had been established, to set up side camps, also called spike or fly camps, as outposts of the main unit. The side camps consisted of a dozen or more men who set up a small tent camp several miles from the main base. They would then spend up to several weeks completing a job near the site. The arrangement saved them the time of traveling long distances back and forth to their work location each day. Equipment, tools and machinery would be delivered to them periodically. A cook would usually be assigned to the side camp, completing the circle of independence from the main unit. For CCC enrollees, the more relaxed duty at a side camp away from the watchful eye of a camp commander was often considered a plum assignment.

Devil's Lake State Park was the site of a CCC side camp in May 1934, over a year before the main camp at the park was built. Twenty-four young men from a state forest unit at Camp Petenwell (S-51) near Necedah, Wisconsin, came in on a temporary assignment that turned into an extended stay. Since the park was an established tourist destination well before the CCC days and had a reasonable complement of amenities, it was not necessary to set up a tent camp for just a handful of men. Instead, they were housed at the old Kirkland Hotel at the southern end of the lake. Their work projects that summer involved some trail work, plus remodeling on two buildings in the park. They also embarked on an ambitious job of raking and cleaning the entire shoreline to make it "practically perfect" for wading and swimming.[21]

Drawing duty at the south shore of beautiful Devil's Lake and sleeping in a regular bed at a hotel was unbelievably good fortune. They knew it was special. Despite the day-to-day work assignments, these men looked around and thought they had died and gone to heaven. Thankfully for the side camp boys, there was enough work around the lake to keep the camp operating until May 1935.

THE CCC ARRIVES
AT THE PARK

Almost two hundred young men of the CCC were headed for Devil's Lake State Park in 1935. They were the new Company 2669. Hometowns for many of these men were Milwaukee, Kenosha and Eau Claire. A significantly large number of recruits were from Illinois, and rounding out the group was a handful of Michigan kids. Less than a year earlier, they had been members of Company 2615. Their first duty assignment had been at Camp Blue Mound near Milwaukee. While there, they were involved in construction of the Honey Creek Parkway and other road-building and landscaping projects.[22] Completion of those projects gave them the experience they would need to tackle similar construction jobs at Devil's Lake.

In the parlance of CCC administrators, Company 2669 was classified as a "junior" company unit. The designation did not mean the men were younger in age compared to other units. It simply meant they were not a military veteran or African American company. When the CCC program was created in 1933, there were political pressures put on President Roosevelt to enroll military veterans from the Great War (World War I) into the new program. The veterans had been denied bonus payment of money for their Great War service, and in the summer of 1932, they organized a "Bonus Army" to go to Washington and demand justice. Their repeated demands for the bonus payment fell on deaf ears during the Hoover administration and later when Roosevelt took office. But President Roosevelt defused the situation by offering the veterans a chance to enroll in the new CCC as a way to ease their economic suffering. Thousands accepted the offer.

A full company photo taken by a professional photographer was a popular souvenir item for the enrollees. Yet a company picture was not taken every year, and some young men were left out. This Devil's Lake portrait was taken near the camp entrance in the late summer of 1937. *Courtesy Richard McDavitt.*

The ECW legislation that created the CCC also contained language that prevented racial discrimination in enrollment and organization of companies. Therefore, many of the CCC companies formed early in the program included a number of African Americans. Later, assigning officers began segregating African Americans into all-black units. The upshot for Sauk County was that neither blacks nor war veterans saw service at Devil's Lake. The junior Company 2669 was all white like most CCC units serving in Wisconsin after 1934.

The first organizational move to get the junior unit headed toward the lake came in June 1935. A month later, an advance team of thirty men from the new company was on the south shore of Devil's Lake checking out the new site. The men were directed toward a tree-studded, level piece of land about a quarter mile southeast of the lake. The park people and local citizens called the area the Pine Plantation, since it was covered with rows of small Norwegian and white pine trees. Despite the trees, the site was a beautiful location with the escarpment of the East Bluff a short walk north of the campsite. The only other problem with the site was that there were no buildings on the property to house the enrollees, who would be arriving in a couple months.

It became standard procedure for the CCC men to live in tents on the site and eat from army mess kits until the main buildings could be constructed.

That way, the men could begin conservation work without having to sit and wait for construction materials to arrive for a permanent camp. It was like this in many CCC locations around the country. Problems were bound to arise.

The Devil's Lake camp had an unusual problem given its location. With the lake at their doorstep, it was ironic that officials needed to worry about drinking water for the camp. Yet the camp was intended to be as self-sufficient as possible. Therefore, a few months before any CCC enrollees arrived at Devil's Lake, local bids were sent out for someone to drill a well at the campsite. Few people expected any problems finding water near Devil's Lake. Bids were awarded, and drilling confidently began. That first effort struck solid rock and broke the drill bit. This happened about the same time that the advance team of enrollees showed up. A small group could make do by hauling water the short distance from the south shore to the campsite. However, the full company of two hundred men was coming, and something more permanent had to be done. With a week to go before the entire company was due to arrive, and with the drill depth at three hundred feet, there was still no water. The well drillers were still at work when the full CCC company arrived in early August 1935. Camp commander F.M. Doran hastily arranged for water to be hauled from the Chateau Building on the north shore and made it known that construction of permanent buildings could not begin until the camp had its own well. Shortly thereafter, well water flowed into the camp and the crisis was over. But the incident is an example of the kind of things that happened when a CCC camp was first organized and how commanders had to deal with situations on the fly. It was also a lesson in how enrollees had to adapt.[23]

The tent city at Devil's Lake, circa 1936. For several weeks prior to permanent camp buildings, enrollees lived in tents lined up in a "company street." There is some evidence to suggest that camp commanders made use of the tents as more comfortable summer accommodations even after the permanent barracks had been constructed. *Courtesy Wisconsin DNR, Devil's Lake State Park.*

Prior to the water crisis and the arrival of the full unit, the Devil's Lake enrollee advance crew arrived with up to three dozen huge tents, including a mess tent. It took less than a day to identify company "streets" and locate and dig a latrine. Preparation of mess kit meals was adequate, but without proper kitchen facilities, cleanup was a disgusting chore. After every meal, the enrollees would line up on each side of a table. At the end of the table were a garbage can and two large cooking pots. The enrollee would approach the garbage can first, scraping off loose food from his mess kit into the can. He would then step up to the first pot filled with very hot, soapy water. He would dip his mess kit into the soapy water and swirl the pan to get it clean. That step was usually a quick pass given the extremely hot water. Next, he would step up to the last pot filled with very hot, clear water. Dipping his mess kit in this water was supposed to wash off the soapy residue from the previous rinse. Drying was the last step. The process was done in assembly line fashion, with the water being changed when it either became too cold or the color began to change. No wonder the men were eager to see a permanent mess hall and kitchen under one roof.

With the well water problem solved and the full company at the site, building materials for a permanent camp began to arrive. Few CCC boys had useful job experience in construction, so local labor from Baraboo was used for skilled tasks such as wood framing, plumbing and electrical work. For example, the local economy got a slight boost when the CCC hired twenty-five carpenters from the Sauk County unemployment office to help with building construction at the camp.

Special care was taken to make sure the young men had clean and comfortable (albeit Spartan) living conditions. Enrollee barracks buildings resembled spotless military quarters with rows of single beds lining each wall and a central walkway. Each barracks building could sleep about forty or fifty men. Inspections for cleanliness were common, and the men were required to maintain a neat and orderly area around their beds, which included their personal footlockers. Barracks were heated by two or more wood- or coal-burning stoves. An enrollee "night guard" was assigned to make the rounds and be sure there was enough heating fuel to last until morning.

Outside, military-style groundskeeping was obvious. Crushed gravel and cinders donated to the camp by the railroad were used for sidewalk material between buildings, and the walkways were lined with small, uniformed-sized rocks. Young evergreen trees were positioned all over camp, with small grass

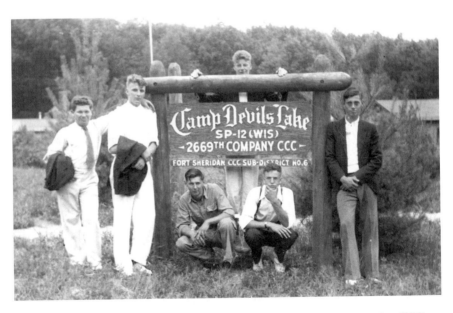

The camp entrance sign was more decorative and unique than that of many other CCC camps, suggesting that Company 2669 employed more time and work in its design. The sign at all camps became an enrollee favorite for picture taking. *Courtesy Wisconsin DNR, Devil's Lake State Park.*

lawns in between. Everyone was asked to contribute, even in the smallest way. The camp newspaper politely called on the boys to use the walkways "and give the grass a chance."

The camp commander was an army officer, usually a lieutenant or captain from the reserve ranks. Another junior officer would assist him. They were in charge of the men while they were in the camp. Obviously, the day-to-day routine was patterned on army life, mindful of the fact that CCC enrollees were not members of the military. There was roll call, KP duty, inspections, camp cleanup and other army-type rules. Politicians and social commentators wondered if the CCC would turn into a quasi-military unit instead of a conservationist program. In addition, the military aspects of life in the CCC were sore spots to many potential enrollees, especially in the early years. Incidentally, there is little evidence that parents objected to putting their sons through a period of military-style discipline.

Jim Mitchell was a runaway teenager from Kenosha, Wisconsin, who had been living the hobo life by hitching rides on freight trains before he saw the light and joined the CCC. In talks around the campfire, Jim's traveling buddy, Peter Lijinski, thought the CCC was a great idea, but Jim was wary. They discussed it further and weighed the options. Jim said, "I balked at the idea of having some army guys push me around…Little did we realize that this stark encampment was the haven thousands of boys like ourselves needed."[24]

Jim served at a state forest camp (S-86) in northern Wisconsin and was never assigned to Devil's Lake. But his introduction to camp routine is similar to the experiences of other enrollees—many at Devil's Lake:

> *I found out what discipline was all about…the camp held inspections every morning. Your bunk had to be neat. You had to be able to bounce a quarter off your blanket. Your footlocker had to be in a precise place. There had to be no dust on your shoes. If you failed inspection, when you got off work that day you would have extra duty.*

Another recruit remembers that at Devil's Lake in 1940, some inspections were unannounced:

> *We would be lying in our bunks listening to the radio, and someone would come into the barracks and tell us there was to be an immediate inspection. We had to hurry up and straighten things out and stand next to our bed as the officers came by. They made sure we were dressed properly, as well as making sure our gear was in order.*[25]

The CCC Arrives at the Park

Despite the military routine, word of the CCC at Devil's Lake spread and no doubt had an impact on young men desperate for work during the Depression years. "My family lived in Portage, not far from the lake. During the Depression nobody had any money or jobs. My father, Emil, did all kinds of things to make money. He was a fine handyman," remembers Bruce Budde.

> *He was a baker, and then a painter for a while. He also worked for the boat works that made launches that the tourists took to visit the Dells on the Wisconsin River. I had an older brother that was deaf and was at the state school in Delavan. I also had a younger brother and sister. I quit high school so I could help my father. I wanted to do something to help out and help make our payments.*

Young Bruce had been hearing about the CCC for some time. By 1940, a large number of young men had gone through the program and had brought home success stories and a new outlook on work and maturity. Bruce even knew a couple of CCC kids who were working in the camp office at Devil's Lake. "I had a couple of cousins who worked there, too," Bruce remembers. Things weren't getting any better around Portage, so Bruce got to thinking, "Why don't I go over there, join up and help Pa out? At least I wouldn't be home eating." For Bruce, it was a decision he made on his own, but his father was initially opposed and thought it best if his son stayed at home. There was no telling where Bruce would be assigned. There was a chance he could be sent out of state. But during the sign-up procedure in Portage, Bruce was given a choice of camp assignments. He could go to Devil's Lake or Rib Mountain State Park near Wausau in the north-central part of the state. Of course, Devil's Lake was much closer, and therefore he would be able to spend weekends at home. It was an easy decision, and one that made Emil Budde feel a little better.[26]

Thirty miles southwest of Portage, also located on the Wisconsin River, were the twin communities of Sauk City and Prairie du Sac. From the farmland north of town, one could see the Baraboo Hills. Nestled out of sight in the hills was Devil's Lake. Clarence Guetzkow lived with his family on one of the farms north of town. "Times were tough. I didn't go to high school because Dad said it was more important just then to help out on the farm." Like Bruce Budde, Clarence had heard about the CCC at Devil's Lake and knew two people who were serving there. Clarence's father knew about the CCC also and its record of success. He began to have a change of heart.

"Dad thought it would be a good experience and he more or less pushed me into it." The enrollment period was only six months. The money coming in from his service there could be put to good use on the farm. Maybe he should give it a try. Clarence and several of his Sauk County friends signed the papers. In April 1940, they reported to the CCC camp at Devil's Lake State Park. That same month, Bruce Budde arrived at the camp by the lake. Both boys were eighteen years old and away from home for the first time.[27]

For Budde and Guetzkow, the camp was more like a job site rather than a distant forest assignment. Home for them was not far away. Of course, they had to stay at camp during the workweek, but they could and did get weekend passes to go home. Yet there were only a handful of lucky enrollees like Budde and Guetzkow. For those enrollees coming greater distances, the camp had a slightly different meaning. For them, it was truly a home away from home. Some enrollees even likened it to a boarding school. Indeed, the camp appeared to have all the same features. All permanent camps had up to four long barracks buildings for the enrollees, plus a separate bathhouse. There was also an administration building near the main entrance to the camp. Other buildings included army officers' quarters, a mess hall, a recreation building, an infirmary, a latrine and a garage and workshop for vehicles and equipment. Viewed from afar, one could see the water tower and camp flagpole. The commanding officer acted as the principal, while the technical staff became the teachers. To enhance the experience, perhaps it was better for the young men to think of the CCC that way rather than drawing comparisons to a military base.

What visitors saw in 1937 as they drove up to the entrance of Devil's Lake CCC camp. *Courtesy Richard McDavitt.*

The CCC Arrives at the Park

Another challenge for new recruits involved lessons in the social graces. Simply getting along with two hundred other young enrollees amounted to a big adjustment. Beyond their various school experiences, close quarters living was a new experience. City kids mixed with farm boys, living amongst strangers, was just one of the conditions that had the potential to result in confrontational situations. Disagreements led to pushing incidents and occasional fistfights, but those were rare and dealt with promptly by the camp commander. Other situations were less physical and more a matter of adjusting to group living.

Clarence Guetzkow recalls that in 1940, "a group of guys from Hamtramck, Michigan, reported to camp. Even after they had been here for a while, they pretty much stuck together. They were a little hard to get along with because they thought they were above the Wisconsinites that were here."[28] Devil's Lake also had a large number of enrollees from Illinois. It was not unusual to boast about state allegiances and engage in friendly and informal competition between groups. Such things happened at CCC camps all over the country. It is also true that those geographic differences rarely caused problems in camp. However, the example shows that there was a need for a leadership position that could deal with low-level disagreements.

CCC administrators in Washington discovered this and soon realized that another important level of leadership was necessary: an enrollee leader. As the name suggests, an enrollee leader came from the ranks of the young men themselves and was not a member of the military or technical services. Created during the first summer of operation in 1933, a camp could have several enrollee leaders. Their job was to serve as mentor, dispute umpire and advisor to the recruits. Before an enrollee problem was reported to the army commander, it was often given to the enrollee barracks leader. There was at least one enrollee leader for each of the four barracks buildings at a typically constructed camp. Verbal conflicts, pushing incidents and bunk assignments were often handled first by the barracks leader. Outside the camp, enrollee leaders also acted as second in command at the job sites, helping the technical service foreman teach construction skills. Understandably, the leadership position was usually given to a long-serving enrollee who had "been around" and knew the camp routine and rules. The position was akin to a sergeant in the army, and as a reward, the leaders got paid a few extra dollars. Another benefit was that being a camp leader meant the opportunity to extend one's CCC enlistment past the two-year maximum. That was an important consideration when the job prospects back home remained dismal. But for a young man maturing in the CCC service, perhaps more significant than all of that was knowledge that the CCC issued military-style chevron patches that leaders could wear on their dress uniforms.

Devil's Lake enrollee leaders pose with the job foreman (back row, right). This causal snapshot by enrollee Art McDavitt includes two people in dress uniform with leadership chevrons on their shirtsleeves. *Courtesy Richard McDavitt.*

Camps were also assigned a military doctor. Like the camp commanders, they came from the ranks of the army reserve. Ideally, one medical officer would be assigned to one camp. In 1936–37, a medical officer was stationed at Devil's Lake, but shortly thereafter plans changed. It became impractical to have a military physician on permanent duty at a single camp, so CCC administrators decided to employ "contract" doctors. Dr. Melvin Huth's duty at Devil's Lake serves as a good example of how it worked.

Huth was a medical graduate from the University of Wisconsin–Madison. In 1936, he began private practice in Baraboo, just a few miles north of the park. However, he was also a medical reserve officer, and in 1939, the military called on him to serve as doctor to the CCC boys at Devil's Lake. He could still practice medicine in Baraboo, but every weekday morning at 7:00 a.m. he was at the camp for sick call. He would take care of whatever doctoring was necessary and then return to town to resume his regular practice. However, he was still on call for any emergencies at the camp. Those with minor ailments were left in the care of an enrollee who had emergency training and certification in first aid. Serious cases were removed to a regional hospital or even to a medical facility near the district headquarters in the Chicago area. For Huth and other contract doctors, their duty usually lasted a year or so before they were rotated out.

All permanent camps had an infirmary/dispensary building or used part of another building for housing the sick. A few beds and basic medicines were available for mild illnesses, overseen by the enrollee orderly. Enrollee David Rouse was at Devil's Lake in the early days and remembers that if a person was sick,

> *you were excused from work, but you couldn't go back to the barracks. You had to lay in all day under the watchful eye of the camp's medical personnel. Unless an enrollee was really ill, he was far better off to go out and do his day's work. At Camp Devil's Lake, nobody used "sick bay" service unless they really needed it.*[29]

Rashes, cuts, colds and sore throats were ailments that kept the dispensary operational. Clarence Guetzkow was glad the dispensary was available when, in 1940, he suffered second-degree burns on both hands as a result of his KP duty:

> *It seemed like I was washing dishes all day long. I think it was the combination of very hot water and harsh lye soap that made it bad. Anyway, Dr. Huth put salve on my hands and wrapped them in bandages. I spent a week or so in the dispensary.*[30]

Such stopgap treatments were necessary, effective and comforting for the men, who knew that facilities and care were available on-site to handle accidents.

On occasion, a medical emergency would overwhelm the dispensary and close the entire camp. In late January 1936, the Devil's Lake camp was under quarantine for scarlet fever. A little over a week after that, smallpox concerns kept things closed up, with specific instructions to avoid Baraboo.[31] It is unclear if the dreaded illnesses were real or just a more common contagious condition that was running through the camp. Nonetheless, camp commanders and doctors took few chances with such things. Sometimes, fewer than three men with a common condition would be cause to close the camp.

Quarantine measures were common during the winter months. During such quarantines, it was a rare event if the situation became urgent enough to remove patients to area hospitals. At Devil's Lake, the worst of it seemed to hit in February 1939, when forty-one enrollees were stricken with influenza. That number represented almost 25 percent of the camp population. Commander H.D. Davidson followed the usual procedure. Inoculations were given, men were separated and the crisis passed with a few days of bed rest.

There was another element of camp life that went beyond conservation work. It was President Roosevelt's directive that the CCC also enhance the maturity and well-being of the men. Therefore, each camp had a person who served as an education advisor. This person was not a CCC enrollee; rather, he was a contract worker similar in nature to the camp doctor. Oftentimes, this person was a teacher from the local community. His primary duty was to offer classes that met a specific need for his men or taught them a skill or job that would help them when their enlistments expired and they went home to find work. If the advisor had the skills, he could teach the class himself. Otherwise, he had a member of the technical services take over, or on some occasions, a talented enrollee could lead a class.

The standard offerings were classes dealing with common academic subjects such as basic math, geometry, physical science and history. Enrollees nationwide used these classes to complete school at all grade levels. However, thousands more faced the embarrassing fact that they could not read or write. Their letters back home were ones that were dictated to barracks buddies who wrote and mailed the letters for them. Therefore, reading and writing classes were offered as an option by the education advisors in almost all camps. An enduring legacy of the CCC was that thousands of young men learned to read and write as part of their camp experience.

The education advisor also offered vocational training classes that were especially popular with the men. The specific kind of classes offered often depended on the results of polling conducted by the advisor. Among the favorites were mechanical engineering, air conditioning and vehicle maintenance. Other more informal classes, not part of vocational training, were also offered and were very popular with the men. They included woodworking, public speaking, leatherwork and photography. The sign-up sheet for all classes was posted around the camp, with most meetings taking place in the evening to avoid work conflicts. The education advisor was also responsible for the camp library and recreation room.

Oftentimes among enrollees, the education advisor was the most popular and trustworthy adult at the camp. Unlike the military officers, work foreman and other members of the technical crew, the education advisor had no legal authority over the men. He did not wear a uniform and could not order the boys about or require them to attend class. Rather than looking down on those factors, many enrollees viewed education advisors as confidants. As a civilian, many of the enrollees came to him for advice or problems that were too embarrassing to tell other adults, including those problems their barracks leaders were unable to work out.

Above: Education advisor W.R. Winkelmeyer in 1937, doing his part to keep the camp clean. *Courtesy Richard McDavitt.*

Right: Education advisor Anthony Heibl at LaValle (WI) CCC camp in 1937. He would later take over from Winkelmeyer at Devil's Lake. As a civilian hired by the CCC, the education advisor was the only nonmilitary adult at camp in whom the young enrollees could confide about personal matters. *Courtesy of Bill and John Heibl.*

There were a number of education advisors at Devil's Lake throughout its camp history, and all apparently did a fine job, but two seem to stand out. William R. Winkelmeyer was the first. Aside from his usual duty of organizing classes for the men, he was known to put together field trips for the boys (more on that later) to special historical or job-related locations. The trips were not required as part of Winkelmeyer's job, and unless required as part of a class, attendance was optional. But Winkelmeyer didn't have to worry about no-shows. Enrollees soon came to realize that the trips were often the most popular and rewarding events on the weekend, and space on the vehicles leaving camp filled quickly.[32]

In 1938, Anthony J. Heibl came to Devil's Lake as education advisor. Heibl's story is a common example of what CCC administrators were looking for when they hired a camp education advisor. He had teaching

credentials and the academic background that went with it. He knew how to organize classes and conduct meetings. An additional plus for Heibl (and almost certainly the reason he got the job over other applicants) was that his physical education training was useful in promoting the ever-popular camp sports activities.

Heibl was very active in all aspects of the camp sports program—another routine part of the advisor's job. But once again, the Devil's Lake advisor went the extra mile. He was the coach of the basketball team and, in addition, ran the intra-barracks basketball competition. For the barracks tournament, he acted as the referee. Thinking about how his court rulings would affect

Enrollee Frankie Culetta getting in some practice after work. Sports were such a big part of CCC life that camp commanders at Devil's Lake arranged for gymnasium space in Baraboo as winter weather made outdoor games impractical. *Courtesy Richard McDavitt.*

Precision in job performance was a function of proper instruction and practice. Education advisors and adult craftsmen were the keys to properly training young men in the construction trades. *Courtesy Wisconsin DNR, Devil's Lake State Park.*

his enrollee relationships, Heibl remarked, "Here's where I find out who my friends are."[33]

The examples of Heibl and Winkelmeyer are representative of the impact that the education program had on CCC youth. Roosevelt's desire to use the CCC opportunity to build intellectual maturity through education, as well as physical maturity through hard work, was largely successful because Winkelmeyer's and Heibl's dedicated service was repeated in camps all over the country.

At Devil's Lake and elsewhere, project foremen and supervisors from the camp technical staff joined with the education advisors to offer "off-the-job" classes consistent with their daytime work assignments. Before and during big projects, it was customary for foremen and supervisors to meet with enrollees and talk about the tasks the young men would perform. In addition, night classes went above and beyond the skills they picked up during the workday. Examples included masonry and concrete, plumbing, surveying and landscape forestry. All of those advanced skills could be practiced later as part of the daily work projects at the job site. In addition, certificates of completion were issued to enrollees finishing selected classes and passing a skills exam. The certificates verified certain skills training and were treasured by the enrollees because the document could be used to enhance employment prospects when the young men left to find work in the civilian world.[34]

3

DAILY LIFE AT THE CAMP

Getting used to the camp routine was an important part of an enrollee's life. Since the U.S. Army controlled the routine at the camp, most everything there was done "the army way." It was barracks-style living with no private rooms for enrollees. The *CCC Handbook*, given to incoming recruits, was an orientation guide that sought to answer questions that might arise about life in the camps. In part, it read, "You will have to learn to get along in a friendly way with all the other fellows...Some of them have different faiths and opinions and attitudes and temperaments from those you are used to."[35] Most recruits did not present a problem. Many young men away from home for the first time were too scared and intimidated to even consider breaking the rules. Others joined for the express purpose of being around people their own age, making new friends and getting along with others. There were only a relative few who wanted to make an impression on their fellow bunkmates by seeing how far they could bend the rules and demand attention.

During the week, the men were awakened about 6:00 a.m. and used the time before the morning meal to make their beds, dress and get ready for a day's work. Breakfast was at 7:00 a.m., and by 7:45 a.m., they were expected to be outside ready to work. At Devil's Lake, NPS supervisors and work foremen met the enrollees in the front parking area with trucks ready to drive them to the job site. Occasionally, work would be close enough to camp for the men to simply walk to their job assignment. By 4:30 p.m., workers were on their way back to camp, and the evening meal was served during the five o'clock hour. After dinner, enrollees had the rest of the night to themselves. Lights out at the camp came at 10:00 p.m.[36]

Part of the daily routine at Devil's Lake. Enrollees begin to form up outside their barracks buildings (right) in preparation for receiving their job assignments for the day. *Courtesy Wisconsin DNR, Devil's Lake State Park.*

Meals were an important part of camp life. Indeed, many enrollees looked forward to getting off work in the afternoon and immediately heading for the mess hall; but it didn't do any good to cut corners and get to the mess hall ahead of the hungry horde. In 1940, Bruce Budde recalls that camp commanders had a loudspeaker at camp that announced, "Chow in five minutes!" as a way to let the mob know when things were ready. Nobody was allowed in before the public-address proclamation. "Guys were ready to eat but had to stay in the barracks until the announcement, but boy, talk about a scramble to the mess hall when the call came."

"We ate good," Budde recalls. This was a common conclusion of recruits almost everywhere. Enrollees felt that the food was truly satisfying and tasty, with lots of variety and choices. Another bonus was that the quantity of food available was often beyond what they got back home. Enrollees got their fill at the dinner table because they could often eat as much as they wanted. It was not unusual for young men to leave service in the CCC healthier and heavier than when they came in. An endless supply of coffee, a meat dish of some kind and a choice of desserts seemed to be the key to keeping everyone happy. But there was more to it than that.

While cooks were also enrollees, many came from restaurant backgrounds, and all attended a "Cooks and Bakers School" prior to being turned loose

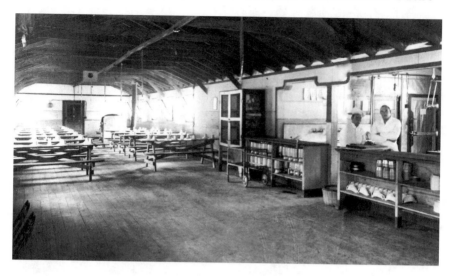

The Devil's Lake mess hall as it looked just before mealtime in 1937. Kitchen cleanliness was a top priority of camp commanders. *Courtesy Richard McDavitt.*

in the camp kitchen. Cooks, bakers and other kitchen staff did not rotate to other duties or work on outdoor conservation projects like the rest of the men. Their full-time job was to stay in camp and prepare meals. With work at Devil's Lake confined to the park, it was easy on many occasions for the men to return to camp for a hot lunch in the mess hall. Indeed, it was often the case that the noon meal (called dinner) was more varied and appealing than the evening supper. For example, the following is the Devil's Lake menu for July 3, 1936:

Breakfast—Oatmeal, oranges, creamed beef, milk, bread and coffee

Dinner (noon)—Salmon loaf, browned potatoes, buttered peas, apple and celery salad, bread, chocolate cake and coffee

Supper (evening)—Chili con carne, crackers, coleslaw, green onions, bread, cookies and iced tea

CCC district administrators in Illinois contracted for much of the food at Devil's Lake and had it shipped to the camp via rail or truck convoy. However, camp commanders contracted locally for some items such as fresh fruits and vegetables and ice cream from merchants in nearby Baraboo. Reports from Devil's Lake note that even during the difficult days of winter, "the army...

continued to feed consistently well, which perhaps was the greatest source of satisfaction to [park] personnel and enrollee alike."[37]

At the CCC camp at LaValle, the Sauk County sister camp to Devil's Lake, mess sergeant Joe Sweet kept track of what it took to feed a company of young men for one day. He estimated that 220 pounds of meat was necessary, along with 200 pounds of potatoes, 100 loaves of bread, 30 dozen eggs and 20 gallons of milk. Of course, the Devil's Lake company was the same size as the LaValle group, so it is safe to conclude that the food requirements at the lake for one day were similar to those inventoried at the LaValle camp.[38]

Even though food was a big part of an enrollee's life, one of the most dreaded words in the service came from the kitchen: KP. Kitchen Police (or Kitchen Patrol) was required of all enrollees. Regular duty in the kitchen usually lasted one week before a new crew would come in. Each day started with a wake-up call about 4:30 or 5:00 a.m. While the other enrollees slept, the KP crew of about six reported to the mess sergeant. They were given a variety of duties ranging from setting the tables to delivering crates of food to the chefs. The KP crew was generally not allowed to actually cook any of the meal items, although on occasion they were asked to watch a boiling pot. After the meal was over, the KP crew washed, dried and stacked plates and utensils for the next meal. At that point, many newcomers to KP duty thought they would get a break. It was not to be. After breakfast, the mess sergeant had them preparing food (including peeling potatoes) for the

Members of the KP crew peeling potatoes behind the mess hall. While this 1938 photo was taken at a CCC camp in northern Wisconsin, the scene was repeated at Devil's Lake and all other CCC units around the country. *Courtesy U.S. Department of Agriculture, Forest Service. Chequamegon-Nicolet National Forest (WI).*

noon meal. After the noon cleanup, it was time to prepare for supper. They worked through the evening meal and cleanup long after the other enrollees were relaxing in the recreation room or barracks.

Besides the regular KP rotation, enrollees also knew they could be assigned extra KP duty for rules infractions around camp or misbehavior at the job site. Enrollee Bruce Budde remembers that "everybody obeyed the mess sergeant." Bob Karow was not the mess sergeant at Devil's Lake, but he was the chief cook and therefore commander of the kitchen at SP-12. Over six feet tall with a square jaw and a muscular, athletic body, Big Bob had no trouble enforcing rules and food preparation assignments among the KP crew. So dreaded was KP that the young men offered other enrollees a dollar a week to take their place in the kitchen.[39] It was a princely sum considering the fact that enrollees got to keep just five dollars for a month's worth of labor in the field.

KP duty obviously took time away from more relaxing pursuits. Off-duty time was special for the young enrollees, and they didn't want to waste it in the kitchen. For those not working in the mess hall, there was always plenty of time to relax in the evening. Reading, letter writing and barracks card games were common pastimes, especially during the confinement of the winter months. Even simple pleasures were worth remembering. Enrollee and Wisconsin farm boy Ted Rozinski remembers the times he could use the evening hours to sit in a comfortable chair in the recreation room and listen to the radio. It was a thrill, he said, "because at home we didn't have a radio."

Every enrollee had his own way of using free time. Walter Lahl was more introspective than the rest. He called himself "a simple man" and enjoyed the simple life around camp. Unlike many of his bunkmates, hiking the hills around camp was not on his list of fun things to do. After all, he did enough of that during his regular workday in the park. Most of the time, going into town for the weekend didn't interest him either. There were other ways to get away from it all. His idea of fun during the off hours was to head for the camp library. It was the most comfortable and quiet room at the camp. There, it was possible to escape the daily routine and use one's imagination to travel to a different world. Wally found his escape in the volumes of pulp fiction. "I especially liked to read westerns," he said.[40] It so happened that during this time, western adventure novelist Zane Grey was near the height of his literary popularity. With titles like *Riders of the Purple Sage* and *To the Last Man*, Grey could thank Wally Lahl and thousands of CCC boys like him for putting his escapist fare near the top of the request list at CCC camps all over the country.

In 1940, Clarence Guetzkow made extensive use of the camp library for reasons much different from Lahl's. "Even though my hands were bandaged

The library room at SP-12, Devil's Lake, in 1937. Despite its small appearance, the camp library had access to hundreds of book titles, as well as hometown newspapers and magazines. The library was one of the few private places at camp where enrollees could enjoy some quiet time. *Courtesy Richard McDavitt.*

from my burns in KP, I spend a lot of time in the library," he said. Confined to the camp, the library was a welcome destination for Guetzkow and other enrollees recovering from work injuries. Going to the camp library and reading books and magazines was better than lying around in the infirmary staring at the ceiling.

Clarence Guetzkow may have had the place all to himself during the day when others were out working on projects, but Bruce Budde was at Devil's Lake at the same time as Guetzkow and remembers that the library was one of the three most popular destinations after the boys finished their evening meal. The library subscribed to several local newspapers and often included papers from the enrollees' hometowns. A camp bulletin board was also located in the library, posting current announcements about classes, town events and matters of general interest. "We went to the library a lot after work," he said. Some days, it was crucial to get a spot at the reading room before anyone else did. The adjoining recreation room was bigger, but it was also noisier. For enrollees needing quiet time, a seat in the library reading room was the best.

Another place to get away from the usual routine was the camp canteen. The canteen was a popular destination because it was so different from the other buildings at camp. Indeed, it wasn't a work building at all. It was a small general store, complete with a display case and counter. Most often, it was operated by the enrollees with profits earmarked for special camp needs. The store contained items for sale that were not part of the CCC standard issue. Those items included razor blades, tobacco, candy, soda pop, toothpaste and other personal items. Enrollee David Rouse said, "My favorite indulgence was a bottle of Pepsi-Cola, a Powerhouse candy bar and maybe a Milky Way." The entire purchase costs David less than twenty cents. Walter Lahl remembers, "I could buy comic books there for ten cents each. I would get a bundle and take them back to the barracks. They were lifesavers later on when I had time to read." Though not open at all hours, the canteen was still a great way to spend time (and what little money enrollees had) in a relaxed and casual atmosphere.

Another camp structure that was used for leisure activities was the carpentry building. It became a favorite wintertime location for those who wanted to tinker with woodworking projects. Plates, cups, toothpick holders and other odd items kept the boys busy during the cold months and also provided gifts for the folks back home. Bruce Budde spent his days working in the carpentry building in 1941 as part of his regular duty but also came in after hours to get things done just for himself. "I liked woodworking," he said, "and I liked to work on things others were not doing."

The camp canteen at Mount Horeb (WI) CCC camp. The Devil's Lake canteen would have looked very similar. Enrollees stocked the counter and shared in the profits. *Courtesy Louis Roedell.*

Daily Life at the Camp

Oftentimes, the young men organized their own projects to pass the time. In April 1940, the boys organized a camp horseshoe tournament as a way to celebrate the end of the winter season and the beginning of outdoor recreation. Horseshoes was a popular pastime at almost all camps because it was simple to set up, and most enrollees knew the rules. It was also a contest in which games could be played during breaks at camp or after the evening meal. At Devil's Lake, the tournament's coming at the end of a long winter of confinement may have had a lot do with its appeal. Over one-third of the enrollees signed up to participate, making it one of the most popular competitions ever organized at the camp. Enrollees eagerly anticipated potential matchups as others were eliminated. A chart was posted in the canteen showing upcoming matches and the names of winners and losers leading to the final championship game.[41] Unfortunately, the name of the 1940 tournament winner has been lost. It hardly matters, however, since the competitors weren't playing for prize money. Bragging rights for the champion was the only reward.

The ultimate fun at the park was invariably tied to the lake. Devil's Lake was about one-quarter to one-half mile from the camp and was a tempting destination after work. Knowing this, camp commanders kept a wary eye on off-camp activities. No person could just simply leave camp when his workday was finished. Permission sign-outs were necessary, and the commanders only allowed a small number of leaves each day. Commanders also wanted to know where in the park the men were going. Travel into Baraboo was frowned upon during the week, and its distance from camp was a factor that worked against the enrollees. There just wasn't enough time to walk into town at the end of a workday and get back in time for lights out. Privately owned enrollee cars were forbidden in camp, and hitchhiking was also against the rules (plus it was unpredictable and potentially dangerous). Use of government vehicles for such trips during the week was out of the question.

Enrollee Clarence Guetzkow developed a routine. When he could manage a pass at the end of a workday, he would walk the short distance west to the lake. "I found the railroad tracks and followed them to the north shore. From there I went to the Chateau to find out what kind of entertainment was being offered." The route Clarence followed in 1940 was the Oregon Trail of CCC enrollees at the park. Ever since the early side camp days of 1934, the young men had followed the tracks north to the park recreation center known as the Chateau. Veteran enrollees guided the newer recruits along the railroad trail year after year. The young men would often pass one another coming and going, trading advice on recreation opportunities

The Chateau as it appeared in the 1920s. Often remodeled in later years, the Chateau was the recreation center for park visitors and CCC boys. The facility was especially popular as a dance venue in the summer. *Courtesy Robert J. Moore.*

as they went. Key travel advice on this trail was to watch the ground so you didn't stumble on the railroad ties. Even better advice was to listen for oncoming locomotives and be prepared to quickly get out of the way.

Making your own fun was part of life in the CCC. The crew at Devil's Lake was fortunate because it had more options than most camps in the Midwest. But sometimes the choices were hard to understand. After a hard day outdoors, for example, who would want to get additional exercise? Enrollee Bruce Budde remembers that "some nights after work a bunch of us would cross the road in front of our camp and follow the trail up the bluff just for something to do." It was all part of making your own fun and better than lounging away the evening on a barracks bunk. Still, enrollees like Walter Lahl could never understand the attraction.

Among all recreational activities, by far the favorite participation sport at camps across America was baseball. At Devil's Lake, the young men embraced the sport with gusto. They began by organizing both a regular baseball team and a separate softball team. The boys constructed two baseball fields near camp and joined a league with competition against other CCC units in the area, plus teams from the nearby towns. Games were played on weekends in order to avoid work conflicts. There were dozens of enrollees who wanted to play but couldn't make the league teams at the camp. To deal with that situation, enrollees put together teams from the different barracks buildings at camp and played against one another. Team standings and scores of barracks games got their proper due in the camp newspaper, alongside the "varsity" team.

Successful teams and players achieved celebrity status and regularly made the camp newspaper. Devil's Lake had its share of winners. In September 1936, the softball team won the district championship with a dramatic late-inning home run by enrollee Stanley Demski. In May of the same year, Big Bob Karow struck out seventeen batters en route to a 17–0 victory over sister camp LaValle. The achievement rated a special mention in the paper's "Chronological History of Company 2669." Despite Karow's achievement, he was not the best athlete in camp. That honor went to baseball slugger, basketball sparkplug and ice-skating star Edwin Johnson of Oconomowoc, Wisconsin. Johnson was also a barracks leader at camp, but like many enrollees around the country, he lived for sports and considered other camp duties a temporary diversion from athletic stardom.[42]

Neither sports nor free time in town could top a holiday break. Everyone wanted to go home during the holidays. Yet allowing two hundred young

Socializing at the outdoor bulletin board are (left to right) star athlete Edwin "Slug" Johnson, barracks leader and first sergeant Ralph Clinton, educational advisor William Winkelmeyer and first cook and star baseball pitcher "Big Bob" Karow. *Courtesy Richard McDavitt.*

men to go home at the same time would effectively shut down the camp for days. Thus camp commanders looked to CCC rules but often used their own judgment when granting leave. If an enrollee lived within one hundred miles of the camp, he was usually able to get leave time at least once during the six-month enrollment period. But no matter the distance, holidays generated a flood of requests to leave camp. At Christmas 1936, half of the enrollees requested passes for home. For the Labor Day holiday earlier that year, almost forty of the boys got permission to leave camp and visit relatives. For those enrollees fortunate enough to get leave time, they were still expected to pay their own transportation costs.

Bruce Budde, Clarence Guetzkow and other "local" kids assigned to Devil's Lake in 1940 were the envy of the camp. They could go home every weekend and on all holidays. "The camp commander discouraged hitchhiking, but we did it anyway to get home," said Guetzkow. Nonetheless, watching glad-hearted teens head for home during the holidays was no fun for those who had to watch them go. Camp commanders did what they could to entertain those left in camp. For example, free time was not wasted for those who had to stay at camp that Labor Day holiday in 1936. The remaining boys received passes for the Sauk County Fair in Baraboo.[43]

For those who had to remain in camp during the holidays, every effort was made to make the experience festive. Barracks rules were relaxed, and special dinners were prepared consistent with the season. White tablecloths came out in the mess hall, along with specially printed menus. Turkey with all the trimmings for Thanksgiving and Christmas, cherry pie for Lincoln's birthday and loads of ice cream for the Fourth of July were standard fare for those special days in camp. Still, after the meal was done, the young men thought of the folks back home and what they were doing that day. While waiting for the time to pass, camp-bound enrollees could also think about the benefits of signing up for another hitch. For all those who reenlisted for another six months of duty, their reward was a pass for six days' leave with pay, plenty of time to get home and back—even for the out-of-state boys.

CCC enrollees were not allowed to have personal automobiles at the camp, so it often became necessary for the young men to hitch a ride out any way they could. Considering the ease of travel into and out of Devil's Lake, camp commanders must have thought about ways to prevent disaffected enrollees from leaving camp and hitching a ride home for good. CCC boys all over the country called this kind of desertion "going over the hill," and it happened everywhere. There were a lot of reasons for leaving—none was complicated. Chief among them was plain homesickness.

Christmas dinner, 1936. Camp commanders stand in the center. Holiday passes to go home were given to as many enrollees as possible. For those remaining, every effort was made, given the limited means, to make the occasion special. *Courtesy Richard McDavitt.*

It is safe to say that most of the young men in the CCC had never been away from home for any extended period of time. A lucky few had enrolled with their buddies from home and could rely on one another when they reported to camp, but many more had to go it alone. Individuals who joined on their own were often assigned to fill out existing but depleted company rosters and were placed wherever the need was greatest. The result was that the new recruit was not familiar with the assignment area and did not know anyone when he reported to camp.

When young Walter Lahl of Milwaukee reported for duty at the lake, he knew no one among the two hundred men in camp. The empty feeling was exaggerated by the fact that Wally joined over the objections of his father. "I wanted to be out on my own," he said. "I joined by myself but have to admit that I got lonely at Devil's Lake." Even though Walter was a quiet kid by nature, he turned his attention to getting along and doing his job properly. In time, he found no trouble establishing friendships thanks to a welcoming attitude and a few days of barracks living.[44]

Clarence Guetzkow was proud to say that he got along with just about everyone and never got into a fight or serious disagreement during his enlistment period. However, when he first reported to camp, he heard rumors among the men that camp commander H.D. Davidson was "not a popular man." Enrollee David Rouse viewed Davidson differently, characterizing him as "well-liked" but also admitting, "He made sure that things got done his way. He was the 'steel hand in the velvet glove.'"[45] As part of a large group of independent-minded young teenagers, it was not unusual that an adult authority figure would be looked upon in different ways. Always in military uniform, "Lieutenant Davidson carried himself erect and would walk around camp with this stick [a riding crop or baton] yelling at the guys and slapping that stick. He never hit anybody with it but it made a lot of guys nervous." Clarence never had any discipline trouble with the commander, but trouble or not, the other enrollees noticed Davidson's unusual manner as well. He quickly picked up a whispered nickname around the barracks—"Stink." It is unclear why that nickname was chosen, but it's a good bet that word of the moniker never made it back to Davidson. There was one final insult to the commander's character. To go along with Davidson's military bearing, the commander also sported a small, thin mustache. It earned him a chuckle up and down the barracks and invited comparisons to authoritarian political figures. Guetzkow remembers, "That small mustache made him look like Hitler."

In an ironic reversal months later, an incident outside of camp forced Guetzkow to admit that Davidson had a softer side to his character: "As I was hitchhiking home one day as part of my leave, Davidson and his wife drove by, saw who I was and picked me up." It was a special moment that stayed with Guetzkow decades after the roadside courtesy. "I figured when he was not commanding the boys at camp, he could be a regular fellow."[46]

Despite the occasional grumblings, the Devil's Lake boys knew they had drawn a good assignment. The setting was beautiful. There were plenty of opportunities for interaction with the park visitors, and the welcoming attitude of nearby Baraboo made the CCC experience at Devil's Lake appear much less isolated compared to camp assignments elsewhere.

CCC veteran Emil Pradarelli served at Long Lake (F-29) near Iron River in the heavily wooded and lake-studded part of extreme northern Wisconsin. Winters were long, the spring season was muddy and the pleasant summer weather attracted swarms of mosquitoes. A town with a movie theater was something enrollees could only dream about. In 2004, Pradarelli attended the state-sponsored tribute to the CCC held at Devil's Lake. Later, he was asked if he saw duty at Devil's Lake in his younger days. "No," he said. Then he paused for a long moment, sighed and slowly added, "That would have been nice."[47]

4

BARABOO AND THE BOYS

While many, and perhaps most, new enrollees had only heard about Devil's Lake, it is a good bet that more than a few (especially those from Wisconsin) knew something about Baraboo. Even in the 1930s, Baraboo was no small "burg." It had a population of over fifty-five hundred, and beyond its importance as a commercial center for northern Sauk County farmers, it had an amusement park reputation for leisurely good times. It was not only the tourist gateway to Devil's Lake, but the town was also within easy reach of the Dells of the Wisconsin River. The Dells are a geologic wonder quite unlike the Devil's Lake landscape. The evocative sandstone formations carved by the river in the Dells invite further exploration into claustrophobic side canyons with names like Witch's Gulch and Lost Canyon. Its proximity to Devil's Lake prompted many tourists to take in both locations during the same vacation. Baraboo was in a position to provide accommodations for both destinations.[48]

The relationship between the town of Baraboo and the Devil's Lake CCC camp mirrored a national trend of generally mutual and pleasant gratitude and coexistence. Overriding the uncertainty of having strange young men camping outside one's town was the realization on the part of civic leaders and town merchants that the influx of new neighbors could add a new social element to an otherwise static existence. Of more immediate importance was the knowledge that a camp's operation and work needs could, in time, lift a town out of its economic stagnation.

On a national level, the numbers were staggering. For fiscal year 1938, CCC administrators estimated they would spend $50 million to feed enrollees at roughly two thousand camps nationwide. One million chickens would be needed to supply eggs to the camp. Over fourteen thousand cows were necessary to keep up with milk production for the young men. Another seventy-five thousand cows would supply butter. One hundred thousand acres of land would be needed to produce the potatoes that enrollees would peel in CCC kitchens as part of KP duty.[49] The good news for local producers was that nearly half the food items were perishable supplies—much of which would have to be purchased locally.

A CCC camp was like having a new little town spring up next to one's community. It was a little town that needed food, raw materials for outdoor projects and a multitude of unforeseen items and services that were needed quickly and had to be purchased locally. Even though most nonperishable items were shipped to Devil's Lake from Chicago, the following foodstuffs for the camp were purchased in Baraboo each month: fresh fruits and vegetables, bread, butter, eggs, milk, cheese and fresh beef. That was the food list, but CCC money was spent on other things as well.

A good CCC camp commander always took the first step in reassuring the community members that having a camp near their town was going to be good for them. In late August 1935, with most of the permanent camp buildings complete, Devil's Lake commander F.M. Doran invited 150 Baraboo businessmen to visit the facility. They received a tour of the buildings and a briefing from Doran and others about what kinds of projects the boys would work on. The camp authorities wrapped up the evening by offering "supper, army style," at the camp mess hall. The message to the merchants of Baraboo was twofold. First, the camp would be involved in worthwhile projects in the park that would also benefit local citizens. Second, as part of a fully functional camp for 200 people, regular purchases would have to be made. Many of those spending transactions would take place in Baraboo.

There were many times when camp commanders couldn't wait several days for orders to be processed and shipped. For example, tools and machinery often broke during critical times on the job and needed repair or replacement immediately. In those cases, the camp commander or job superintendent called on local businesses to deliver parts and equipment the same day, resulting in fewer lost work hours. Money spent for these incidental work items (tools, lumber, auto parts, electrical components, etc.) was important for the town and amounted to an average of $200 per month.[50] Such expenditures were necessary each and every month over the life of the camp. Merchants were delighted as thousands of otherwise lost dollars came to the town each year as a result of CCC commerce in Baraboo. This, of course, did not count the modest amount of enrollee wages spent in town.

Of course the camp was always eager to get something back if the opportunity presented itself. The degree to which the camp sought favors from the Baraboo community was a function of how aggressive the camp commander was in asking for assistance. Lieutenant H.D. Davidson commanded Devil's Lake in 1939 and was not shy about asking for certain items for camp use. The spring thaw of 1939 was an especially muddy one at the camp. Enrollees and commanders alike prided themselves on keeping a clean campground, but weather conditions conspired against them. The cinder sidewalks between buildings got heavy foot traffic and quickly became a sticky, soupy mess. Bits of mud and small cinders stuck to the men's boots and were tracked everywhere. There was only one way to permanently beat the mud bog conditions: paving bricks. The commander got on the telephone to the *Baraboo News-Republic*. Was there anyone out there in the community who could part with some old bricks? The next day, two truckloads were on their way to the camp, and shortly thereafter Devil's Lake camp had brick sidewalks. Part of Davidson's success in these matters came from the fact that he knew how to say thank you. He made sure the thank-you message made it into the local papers.[51]

In the meantime, there was a national debate going on in some places about what kind of kids were in the CCC and what could be expected of them. At

Formal inspection at Devil's Lake camp, 1936. Enrollees in dress uniforms wait to be dismissed. Such inspections often took place prior to weekend leaves and came with a warning from the camp commander to behave while visiting a neighboring town. *Courtesy Wisconsin DNR, Devil's Lake State Park.*

one end of the spectrum were those who thought the army way of life in the CCC was turning unsuspecting young people into robotic soldiers. At the other end of the scale were those who thought the CCC was recruiting the dregs of society, and these criminal youths would roam the streets of town looking for trouble. A smaller contingent of folks believed that two hundred inexperienced boys sent into a wilderness or park area would, during the course of their work, destroy the natural environment they were supposed to protect. Since the CCC program was a new national experiment, it took a few years to dispel the various rumors and horror stories that filtered down to Main Street America.

There are several possible reasons why opposition to the CCC did not take root in Sauk County. Perhaps a deciding factor was the fact that Baraboo already had an inkling of what living with the CCC boys would be like. The 1934–35 side camp gave Baraboo a small sample of what it was like having a camp a few miles away. While the numbers at a side camp are no comparison to a fully manned company unit and associated camp building, they were enough to prove to the community that the CCC boys were not a bunch of hooligans.

At Peninsula State Park in Door County, opposition surfaced in part because conservationists feared that improvement projects undertaken by the CCC boys would instead damage the wild areas of their park.[52] That was not a significant consideration at Devil's Lake. For better or worse, the lake had been used as a tourist destination for over seventy-five years prior to the arrival of the CCC and had seen extraordinary development and redevelopment of its shoreline. Railroads, excursion boats, resort hotels, cottages and amusement-park type structures all had made their appearance at the lake before Company 2669 arrived. The area immediately around the lake shoreline (where the most notable CCC projects would take place) was not a wilderness or natural area. Therefore, opposition to CCC work based on environmental concerns was not a credible debating point. The forested area away from the lake did, however, have some wilderness characteristics, but even that could be disputed. It could also be argued that trail work away from the lake would not despoil the wilderness environment but instead preserve it by directing travel along designated paths and keeping people from creating their own pathway where none existed previously. Also, a planned network of trails would simply take visitors in an orderly way to areas of the park that they visited anyway, such as Devil's Doorway.

Initial uncertainty and a reasonable amount of skepticism on the part of townspeople were understandable. In little steps and quiet ways, it became clear that the town and camp could help each other. The community and camp partnership began even before the permanent camp buildings went up. As famous as the camp would become for its construction of the stone buildings, the very first task of Company 2669 upon arrival in July 1935 had nothing to do with masonry and everything to do with classic forest conservation.

The *Baraboo Weekly News* of July 11, 1935, reported that George Reynolds of Portage, Wisconsin, was contracted to drill a well on the site of the camp prior to the arrival of the first group of CCC boys. Upon noticing the three thousand small pine trees at the camp location, which would be an obvious impediment to camp construction, he and camp officials came up with a community-sharing solution. He simply suggested that instead of work crews using axes to clear the trees and make way for barracks buildings, local citizens could place a request order with city officials, come out, dig up a tree and take it home—free of charge. It was a marvelous idea. The CCC boys would deal with the remaining trees after they reported for duty, and construction could begin on the camp buildings without delay. A short time later, the local economy got an additional boost when it was announced that bids for construction of the camp buildings would be open to local builders and contractors.[53]

Part of the Pine Plantation that was integrated into the Devil's Lake CCC camp. The size of the trees suggests that this photo may be from the first winter at the camp, in 1935–36. *Courtesy Wisconsin DNR, Devil's Lake State Park.*

Keeping with the conservation mission of the park service, Company 2669 carefully uprooted most of the remaining small trees that were left after the initial giveaway. They were then replanted in the public campsite and picnic ground on the south side of the lake. Other trees were replanted as a screen along the right of way of the Chicago & Northwestern Railroad tracks running along the eastern shore of the lake. Furthermore, many trees were simply left alone at the campsite, to be incorporated into the landscaping of the camp.

Of course, there was a political as well as practical reason why the Pine Plantation was not cleared with axes and saws. The motive seemed to have had as much to do with public relations as with woodland conservation. Even during the Depression years, Devil's Lake State Park remained a very popular tourist destination. Visitors from all over the Midwest could easily see what the CCC boys were doing, and the stories would quickly circulate back home. It would never do to see CCC boys destroying dozens of trees at their campsite, and it would never do to have the citizens of Baraboo think that the first assignment of their CCC neighbors was to clear-cut part of the park.

Evidence of despoiling parkland for the sake of CCC convenience cannot be found in the Baraboo newspapers, the camp newspaper or official reports from district administrators. On the contrary, examples abound about work projects that bent over backward to protect the natural character of Devil's Lake. Chief among them was the rule about no mechanized equipment on trail-building jobs. Such a decision was a commendable rule that was ahead of its time in terms of environmental protection. The downside for the men was that it put more of a physical burden on the CCC workers, who would have to move boulders by hand.

Beyond curiosity, park conservation or city commerce, Devil's Lake and Baraboo established an inevitable social connection with each other. For the enrollees, this connection focused on the weekend. If young people wanted to meet, Baraboo was the nearest and most logical place. City fathers must have blanched at the thought of dozens of young men descending on their community each weekend for an evening of fun. Yet things rarely got out of hand. The enrollees knew that officials would prosecute crime; plus, seemingly minor offenses were cause for immediate dismissal from the CCC and a humiliating reception back home.

Without a lot of money to spend, the CCC boys often settled for the simple pleasures once they arrived in town on a weekend pass. With its twenty-five-cent admission charge, the local movie theater was a popular destination. But there were other social gathering places. Enrollee Clarence

The business district on the Baraboo city square in the 1940s. The city square, and its merchants, was a popular destination for CCC boys during the weekends. *Courtesy Robert J. Moore.*

Guetzkow recalled that "just a half a block off the town square was the Alpine Restaurant. A lot of guys liked to go there because it was easy to strike up a conversation with the waitresses." A less intrusive pastime was the ritual of strolling around the town square window-shopping or maybe sitting on a park bench admiring the young ladies. Many who thought they could get away with it sought out a bartender who would serve them a drink.

The consequences of having a little too much to drink were almost never considered, especially among young men barely out of their teens. In Baraboo, after one night on the town in 1940, Guetzkow remembers a group of enrollees piling into the back of an army truck that would take them back to camp. After leaving town, the road gradually rose in elevation as it approached the lake. The south shore road split from the north shore road and continued uphill, finally cresting, and then descended to the south shoreline. The park road that led downhill to the south shore was narrow and wooded on both sides. That part of the road was nicknamed the "corkscrew" by the men. It was a challenging drive and had to be negotiated carefully even in good daylight conditions. "Our driver was drunk that night," Guetzkow said.

He started down the corkscrew too fast and we were all bounced around in the back of the truck. We didn't know what was going to happen, but suddenly we were at the bottom. How we ever made it back to camp in one piece that night I'll never know.

The truck rolled into the garage area at the opposite end of the camp from the officers' quarters, and the enrollees stumbled back to the barracks in the starlight, vowing to keep things quiet. The incident became a special memory for everyone on the truck and, thankfully for the driver, did not make it into an official report. Such daredevil adventures rarely did.[54]

Perhaps more typical of a Saturday night with the CCC boys in Baraboo was the one chronicled in an article that appeared in the October 15, 1941 issue of the camp newspaper. A dance had been arranged in town that was eagerly awaited by the Devil's Lake men. Such mixers were not uncommon between the young ladies of the town and the CCC boys of the camp. For most, it was the number one social activity of the week.

There was a lot of barracks bragging before the dance, so later the staff reporter found it. . .

a shock to discover that almost all of our big burly muscular men, who tell those fascinating "true experience" stories in the barracks, are really bashful boys…it was odd to see so many of our boys hang back off the dance floor…Those men who…daily work among flying chips of the sharpest stone…going into a state of shock at the mere thought of attempting to dance.

Despite the bouts of shyness, romance often blossomed at local events, and courtships developed. Many an enrollee (and town girl) dreamed of a marriage proposal somewhere in his future after meeting someone at a town dance.

Sunday for the boys at camp was not unlike a Sunday back in their hometowns. While it was a time to relax with friends, get away from camp and enjoy their surroundings, it was usually a dress-up day as well. It was customary for camp commanders (including those at Devil's Lake) to make trucks available to the men who wanted to go into town for church services. Enrollees going to Baraboo for religious reasons in the morning often used the rest of the day to remain in town, either socializing or going to the movies, all the while attired in their dress uniforms.

In a more official capacity, state park rangers were glad the CCC boys were around. They were called to help with emergencies on a number of occasions. Falls and accidents were common occurrences during the height of tourist season, yet most of the problems were not serious and were handled by park employees. At times, however, special help was needed, and the CCC boys responded. Most calls had to do with search-and-rescue efforts. For example, the *Baraboo Weekly News* reported in August 1941 that a young man visiting from Milwaukee (not a CCC man) had fallen while climbing on the Devil's Doorway rock formation and suffered a debilitating injury. He was "brought down from the bluff by CCC men within 45 minutes of the accident...a CCC truck was used to transport him to Baraboo." Over the years, the enrollees became a sort of reserve rescue squad for park rangers. By the time the camp was closed, the boys had participated in recovery operations for drowning victims and numerous searches for lost hikers.

During the years of operation at Devil's Lake, the camp followed a nationwide tradition of a one-day celebration each year commemorating the anniversary of the formation of the CCC. Open house was a time in which camp commanders were determined to put their best foot forward to impress the locals. Keeping the camp clean was always a priority, but before the 1937 open house at Devil's Lake, the enrollees were put to work after they came in from their daytime job assignments. In preparation for visitors, they were instructed to clean up the front reception area, plus the walkways around camp, while another crew applied a coat of paint to walls inside some of the buildings.

The 1937 open house was held in April in observance of four years of national service—two as a permanent company at the park. Much of the intent was designed not only to promote general trust and goodwill but also to peel back the mystery of what was going on at the camp on the south shore. It was the locals' chance to explore a facility that was generally not open to casual visitors—although there was no formal order to that effect. Preparations at Devil's Lake to spruce up the facility and put on the best event possible for the 1937 open house apparently paid off. The Baraboo newspaper reported the affair as "an impressive outdoor program."

The day's festivities opened with a few musical numbers by the gray-and-red-uniformed members of the Baraboo High School band. After a welcoming speech by new camp commander, Lieutenant W.L. Uitti, there was an opportunity to join a formal guided tour of the camp led by army personnel and selected enrollee leaders. Guests were also allowed to roam the grounds freely, inspecting any of the buildings and asking enrollees questions about their work. Later, there were speeches by NPS officials, who summarized the current work projects. At the end of the day, there was dinner

First Lieutenant William L. Uitti, engineers reserve officer, commanded the Devil's Lake camp in 1937. The demeanor of the commanding officer could have a big impact on enrollee morale. During Uitti's year at Devil's Lake, inspectors noted that "enrollees are very contented here." *Courtesy Richard McDavitt.*

for all. Guests, camp commanders and enrollees dressed in their Sunday best. With the meal served in the camp mess hall, the commander announced that, despite the white tablecloths on the long dining tables, the service and food that day was the same the enrollees would eat on any other special occasion or holiday.

After the evening meal, a "private dance" topped off the program. One of the barracks buildings was converted into a dance hall, complete with streamers hung from the rafters. Baraboo's own Lawrence Ott and his Kings of Swing provided the musical entertainment. A 10:30 p.m., an evening brunch was available for those who had worked up an appetite on the dance floor. It was obvious that commander Uitti had pulled out all the stops, offering more entertainment, food and information than many other camps holding open house events. He knew it was a once-a-year opportunity to prove to Baraboo that the CCC was going to continue to be a cooperative business and social partner.[55]

Because the camp was located at a popular state park, there were many visitor inquiries about what exactly was going on there. Visitor requests to tour the property came in both formal and informal communications. Of course, tours and visitors were not allowed to interfere with work, but when convenient, and with a little advance planning, the commanders at Devil's Lake had no difficulty accommodating groups who wanted to get an inside look at the camp. In late 1939, a Baraboo women's club numbering 75 members spent part of the day at the lake. Besides the usual camp tour, the group heard from camp commander H.D. Davidson and national park project superintendent Eugene Odbert Jr. They described the history and objectives of the CCC and specific work projects at the lake. Davidson mentioned that the camp currently had 179 enrollees "from all classes of society." A woman in the audience was overheard to say that "the young men were nice clean-looking boys, a credit to the management." Other women "expressed their surprise at the home-like atmosphere which prevails at the camp." One woman was heard to remark, "Why they even have potted plants growing in the windows." The group later dined with the boys in the mess hall and "had an opportunity to see how deftly meals are handled." The group was served the same fare the enrollees were scheduled to eat that night: salad, tomato soup, pork chops, mashed potatoes, scalloped corn, cherry pie and coffee.[56]

Things were not perfect and not without controversy in the CCC, especially in debates between Washington administrators of the program and local labor unions. One criticism of the CCC program when it began was that the young enrollees were taking jobs away from local workmen in the nearby towns. It was a legitimate concern. President Roosevelt responded by creating other relief organizations to help those workers while keeping intact his program of conservation for young men. However, it became apparent that during the course of a normal workday, the CCC boys needed help from skilled tradesmen. The nature of many outdoor jobs, especially those at Devil's Lake, depended on workmen who had backgrounds in civil engineering, survey work and the various building construction trades. Most young CCCers, many just out of high school, had no idea what it took to put up a building, for example. They were going to need lots of classroom instruction, plus on-the-job training if the CCC projects were to be successful.

The solution was the creation of a new category of CCC worker. These people were skilled tradesmen from the local area who could use their talent and experience to teach and direct the young men on work projects. They were known as local experienced men, but the title was soon shortened to LEM. These people were different from the conservationists and landscape architects who helped formulate building plans. LEMs were electricians, plumbers, carpenters and masons who were at the job site every day. They were not classed as CCC enrollees and were paid at a higher wage rate than the young recruits. These older men acted as work foremen and often taught classes relating to their trades in the evening education program. The number employed at each CCC camp varied depending on the kind of work that was being done. While the number of LEMs hired at each camp was small, somewhere between six and fifteen, there was a larger point to be made. The CCC wanted to show

Edward Bokina, local experienced man (LEM), at work in the park, 1937. LEMs acted as foremen on the job and often performed some of the more technical parts of a work project. *Courtesy Richard McDavitt.*

that it cared about local workers, and the LEM connection was an attempt at local partnership that included modest employment opportunities. While it was largely a symbolic effort to reach out to the towns, the goodwill appeared to have worked. As the CCC program got past its first few years, there was almost no labor union opposition to what the CCC was doing.

Baraboo and Sauk County citizens knew that the CCC and its work projects were a resource that should be courted. Perhaps the ultimate compliment to the Baraboo–Devil's Lake camp partnership came in an understated message from C.B. Hornung, mayor of Baraboo, printed on page one of the March 31, 1938 issue of the camp newspaper:

> *We who live in this community are beginning to realize the value of the established CCC camp at Devil's Lake…By having this camp…it has been possible to make many outstanding changes which will promote greater enjoyment for the public, and preserve for posterity its outstanding beauties. I wish your camp and camp paper future success.*

5

DAVID ROUSE AND THE EARLY YEARS

I can only describe the area as magnificent. It was at Devil's Lake that I first became acquainted with one of Wisconsin's beautiful jewels." Eighteen-year-old David Rouse had just gotten off the train at Devil's Lake State Park. David's experience at the lake would, of course, be unique to him, and he would have his own special memories. Yet what he went through during his tour of duty was common to many young CCCers. Economic hardship, the emotional pull of home, the uncertainty of meeting new people, the prospect of adventure and learning a trade were things many young men thought about as they made their way through the program. David thought about them too.

David Rouse lived in Milwaukee and had just finished high school in 1935. His family had been hit hard by the Depression. His father could only get seasonal work as a construction plasterer, and they were at times reduced to asking for public assistance. "My self-respect and esteem had sunk to an all-time low," David recalls, "and I was desperately seeking a way out, a new beginning, a fresh start far removed from welfare handouts." David was just the kind of young man the CCC was looking for.

How David came to hear about the new agency and his motivation for joining up was representative of tens of thousands of young men in 1935: "I had heard about the CCC from the newspapers, radio and talking to friends...I was certainly eligible for the CCC since my father was on welfare." Simply being eligible was reason enough for most young men, but David also had a lot in common with those young men who had tried to help themselves and had come up empty. "I was heartily sick of searching for jobs that didn't exist in a nation whose unemployment rate stood at an unbelievable 25 percent," he says. The CCC was David's way out.

After enlistment, he was assigned to Company 2669. He was among the first group of young men to report to SP-12 at Devil's Lake. Aside from the scenery at the park, David was most excited about his government-issued wardrobe:

It consisted of two complete sets of clothing (a blue denim fatigue suit for work and an olive drab uniform for dress), three shirts, three sets of underwear, six pairs of white socks, a raincoat, work shoes, brown belt, a black tie and even a 100 percent wool winter coat.

David's excitement was tempered by the fact that much of his outfit was army surplus from World War I. Alterations were in order, but it was up to the enrollees to get them done. Since few young men knew how to use a needle and thread, additional help was needed. David heard around camp that "some astute enrollee learned of a clever seamstress in Baraboo" who could make everything right "for a very reasonable price."

When he first arrived at Devil's Lake, there were no buildings. The camp was a "tent city" while barracks were being constructed. The frightful adventure of riding out a powerful Midwest thunderstorm in a tent was one of his first memories of camp life. So, too, was the loneliness:

Loneliness and homesickness hung over our wooded area like a light fog... Most of us, including myself, had never been away from home before. We were practically city boys, enjoying our first outdoor camping experience.

Many of the boys suffered with their homesickness privately. David recalls:

Late, late at night...I awoke from a deep sleep while still quartered in the army tents. After listening to the sounds of the night—crickets chirping and soft winds sighing in the trees—I suddenly realized what had really awakened me. Someone was softly sobbing in a cot not too far from mine. I never knew who he was. It was harder for some enrollees to be away from their families and those they loved.

Discipline at the camp depended very much on the conduct and disposition of the commanding officer. Life could be so much more enjoyable if the young men and the top brass got along well together. David was lucky: "The captain, a very well-liked, middle-aged army officer, did not maintain a high visibility or an overpowering image, but he made sure that things were done his way." David does remember that camp cleanliness was a big part of the commander's program. "It was very difficult to obtain a weekend pass," he says, "unless your appearance was sharp and enhanced by a haircut. Our camp barber cut hair for a quarter. He was a very busy man."

David soon settled in to the camp routine. The army was in control around camp, and orders had to be obeyed. But the alternative was worse: "The daily routine of camp life was a welcome change from the negative, welfare life that we had been leading." Some camp jobs were rotated, and kitchen police (KP) was the task most dreaded by recruits, but it was one everyone got stuck with before his tour was over. David was glad to complete his turn:

> *We were all required to take turns peeling potatoes or vegetables, washing pots and pans, running the dishwashing machine, being mess hall waiters, or mopping the floor. Cleanliness inspections could earn an enrollee an extra week if Captain Davidson found something he didn't like.*
>
> *Each barracks housed from forty to fifty men and had three huge barrel wood stoves, which kept us comfortably warm in the winter.*

Inside the barracks building at Devil's Lake, 1937. Camp commanders held inspections often and insisted on army-style rules while the men were in camp. *Courtesy Richard McDavitt.*

Guards would come around during the night and keep the fires going. It was the responsibility of the camp commander to make sure enough fuel had been ordered, but it was up to the enrollees to cut the logs to size. Woodcutting duty for the stoves was another bothersome task that David and other recruits had to face over and above their conservation jobs in the park. State park rangers brought the wood into camp, and a rotating group of enrollees was assigned to cut it into manageable pieces for the stove.

David's only injury at camp came during his time cutting wood: "I scraped my arm when a log turned on me during the firewood detail. I needed salve and bandages plus half a day in sick bay." After that, he was back on the job. Rouse doesn't mention any serious injury cases coming through the dispensary. Instead, he recalls the most common accidents from the early days:

> *One enrollee got stung by a large bumblebee while on landscaping detail and ended up with a badly swollen hand. Another recruit sprained his ankle at the gravel pit...Another got into a patch of poison ivy, and he was laid up for two days.*

The kinds of jobs assigned to David outside the camp were varied during his tour to give him experience in many areas, but much of the work was not

Limestone blocks from the quarry are loaded onto wheelbarrows and dumped into the bin, which pulverizes the rock and drops it into the back of the truck. Such work continued during the winter months, when other projects were postponed. *Courtesy Wisconsin DNR, Devil's Lake State Park.*

the kind of noble and glamorous conservation job he had imagined when he signed up:

> *My work detail of about twenty-four men was driven to a large sand and gravel pit, where we hand-loaded trucks all day long, using long-handled shovels. The material was needed for the new bathhouse being built on the north shore.*

Rouse took it all in stride because he knew he would get a chance to work on more exciting projects:

> *Our work schedule was never a humdrum affair. My compadres and I planted trees, dug ditches, landscaping, built the parking lot at the north end of Devil's Lake* [and] *improved and established hiking trails.*

Some of the men looked forward to the adventure and surprise of jobs that took them away from the park. That only happened when special needs elsewhere required their help. David stepped up and volunteered for one of those assignments when the captain announced that people were needed to help fight a forest fire in the northern part of the state near the Brule River.

David Rouse was an enrollee at Devil's Lake when grading for the north shore parking area began in 1936. The CCC-constructed bathhouse can be seen in the center background. *Courtesy Wisconsin DNR, Devil's Lake State Park.*

When the Devil's Lake volunteers arrived at the host CCC camp up north, David got another kind of surprise:

> *As we got out of the trucks, one of the greeters was Clifford, a good friend from Milwaukee. He also had joined the CCC and came up from Camp Riley in the Chequamegon National Forest to help…We had a grand reunion. Far into the night we talked about old times and compared camp life.*

Friendships and camaraderie were a big part of life in the CCC, but on occasion there were some boys at camp who just didn't get along. In those early days at Devil's Lake, David Rouse knew to keep away from Vinnie: "Vinnie was a Chicagoan and so tough that it seemed he could eat wire and spit out nails." Vinnie's specialty was sneaking up on new recruits and using a concealed knife to cut the belt from their trousers. Vinnie thought it was funny, but the young man on the receiving end would often have to be restrained by others from starting a fight. Barracks scuttlebutt about Vinnie and news of the dangerous prank made it way up the chain of command. David recalls, "He didn't last long at Camp Devil's Lake. Vinnie was dishonorably discharged long before his enlistment period was up, and nobody was sorry to see him go."

Like other enrollees, David looked forward to getting a pass and visiting the folks back home. He was entitled to one weekend pass per month. Because he lived in Milwaukee, it was possible for Rouse to make his way home, visit and have time to get back to camp for Monday morning roll call. Of course, rail travel was the easiest mode of transportation out of the park for the young men. But on more than one occasion, the five dollars that enrollees were left with at the end of each month was not enough.

One weekend, David and a buddy starting hitchhiking their way home. They got as far as Sun Prairie, a few miles northeast of Madison. A cold winter day was rapidly turning to night, and highway vehicle traffic disappeared. "The cold wind cut through our CCC uniforms like a knife," recalls David. "Suddenly, seemingly out of nowhere, the Sun Prairie town constable came along and said, 'How are you doing, boys?' I answered. 'Not too good.'" The constable offered them the hospitality of a Sun Prairie jail cell, "and I'm not going to lock the cell door. Just consider yourselves overnight guests of Sun Prairie." Before heading out the next day, David and his friend received a free jailhouse breakfast. David remembers, "To this day there's a special place in my heart for Sun Prairie and a compassionate constable for providing me with a one-time memory that will never fade."

It is certainly a memory that was repeated on occasion in other towns in Wisconsin and elsewhere across America; it's just as certainly the type of humanitarian gesture that is emblematic of the Great Depression.

David served out his enlistment at Devil's Lake and was honorably discharged in 1936, but he was not done with the CCC. Upon returning home, he found life to be "bleak and depressing." He turned around and reenlisted in the CCC, this time being assigned to a soil conservation camp, SCS-20, Camp Ontario, in Vernon County, Wisconsin. Instead of being located in Wisconsin's most popular park, David's new camp was in the middle of a farmer's field. He dutifully completed his enlistment, doing erosion control in the fields, and then went back home.

David returned to Devil's Lake, but only after his CCC days were far behind him. But he didn't forget what the experience meant to him: "I learned how to do many things, much of which helped me in later life. It was a soul-stirring thing to be a part of, to be proud of and to remember." He was "transformed from a 'nobody' into a 'somebody,' reclaiming that elusive something called self-respect and dignity."[57]

6

GETTING THE JOB DONE

Nobody knew more about managing work projects at Devil's Lake State Park during the CCC era than Eugene Odbert Jr. From the drawing board to the last stone in a building, Odbert was the man who knew what was going on with CCC work and where it would take place. His work history at Devil's Lake covers every year of CCC camp operations, except the last one in 1941. He was not only good at his supervisory job but was also a diligent record keeper. He was just the kind of person the CCC needed to manage a successful camp. He was not only well prepared before he went to work at the lake, but he also used his CCC experience after he left to advance a career in public works just a few miles north of the lake at Portage, Wisconsin.

Odbert was born in Minneapolis, but his family soon moved to Sturgeon Bay, Wisconsin, in the scenic northeastern part of the state. Perhaps it was the nearby waters of Green Bay on one side of his new hometown and Lake Michigan on the other side that got him interested in water and engineering. In any case, building construction and its proximity to water became a part of Odbert's life. Even his higher-education schooling was near the water. In 1929, on the eve of the Great Depression, Eugene graduated from the University of Wisconsin–Madison, with its campus hugging the shoreline of beautiful Lake Mendota. His degree was in engineering combined with training as a land surveyor, but his early career would keep him near the water. His start with the CCC and National Park Service began with his appointment as crew foreman at Pattison State Park (SP-11) in northern Wisconsin. He was shortly thereafter transferred to Devil's Lake with a promotion to senior

Eugene Odbert, 1939. As chief project superintendent for CCC work at Devil's Lake, Odbert was responsible for the timing, pace and quality of all building, trail and other conservation projects in the park. *Courtesy Wisconsin DNR, Devil's Lake State Park.*

foreman. Thin, studious and ever precise in his work, Odbert was on duty for the CCC at Devil's Lake months before the arrival of the first enrollees at the park in the late summer of 1935. By June 1936, Eugene had been appointed project superintendent. It was a position of power and responsibility second only to the camp commander. The commander ran the camp, but in terms of CCC project management in the field, there was no one at the lake who had more authority than Eugene Odbert.

Until he left in 1940, Odbert's hand was on everything built in the park during the CCC era. Yet Odbert was neither an enrollee nor a LEM. Instead, he was hired by the National Park Service to recommend and monitor the progress of all work at Devil's Lake. He was therefore not subject to the enrollment and salary restrictions that bound the recruits who worked at the park. He was there for as long as he wanted to be or as long as NPS officials approved his work. He must have done a good job. It turned out that Eugene Odbert's tenure at the lake was longer than any other individual connected with the CCC program at Devil's Lake State Park.

Despite his title, Odbert wasn't the emperor of the park. Others had a say in what was going to be built. The NPS also employed landscape architects, hydrologists, geologists and others to make decisions about building projects at the park—and that didn't include input from state park personnel and politicians at the statehouse in Madison. But Odbert's was a very important voice in the process, especially if the powers that be wanted to know about things such as completion schedules, skills training for the workers, availability of building materials, quality control and possible civil engineering problems at any of the work sites. As project superintendent, he had the power to recommend building projects in the park and negotiate with district administrators and landscape architects over construction location and design. At the same time, he inspected enrollee work at the job sites, ensuring compliance with approved plans, and occasionally taught vocational classes at the camp in the evening. His hometown was Portage, not far from the park, but he was kept so busy that he took up permanent residence along the south shore, a short distance from the camp.

Like so many visitors before him, Odbert was immediately taken with the beauty of the area. While most of his reports to superiors were in a matter-of-fact style, he took time to remind higher-ups why this camp was special:

> [Devil's Lake] *is a natural wonder attracting thousands of visitors each season. Add to this the spectacular geological formations…plus the inspiring beauty of the wooded hills and vales and you have a lure which has pushed to the background many a man's resolution to be back at the office on Monday morning.*[58]

A young man of thirty when he stepped into a leadership role for the NPS, it didn't take long for Odbert to understand the tasks, both political and practical, that faced him. He could see that the limited financial and manpower resources of the state of Wisconsin could not keep up with the demands of tourists for quality facilities at the park. But having the CCC boys around changed all that. Simply put, he said,

> *the chief objective of all projects for this camp is the ultimate development of camping, picnicking, parking, recreational and other areas so arranged as to provide a maximum of convenience and facilities in the limited space available.*

By assuming this responsibility, Odbert also realized that whatever projects the CCC did at the park, they would be carefully scrutinized. Tourists still came to the lake, despite hard times. In 1938, for example, the park received over 500,000 visitors. Odbert's report admits that "because of the popularity of this region, not only the local community but the State at large is viewing with interest the work progress for this camp."[59] What that meant in plain terms was that people were watching, and CCC work at Devil's Lake had better be good.

Devil's Lake State Park
... during the CCC period.

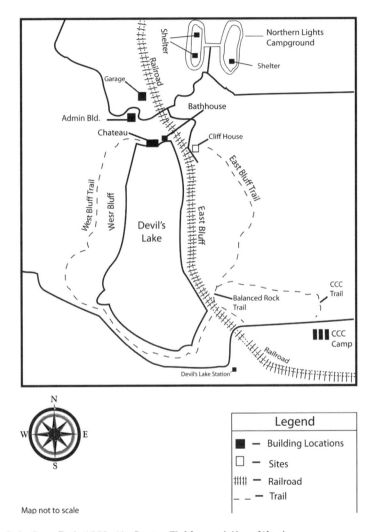

Devil's Lake State Park, 1935–41. *Courtesy Ty Moore and Alyssa Wetzel.*

All work done by Company 2669 was performed exclusively within the boundaries of the state park. Yet much of the work was unseen by the public. Examples include trail building, fire suppression, tree planting and other woodland conservation efforts. But overriding everything were the

Supervisors inspect the main entrance to the bathhouse, 1936. The sign on the right reads, "New Bathhouse. Being constructed under direction of National Park Service, DL. Cooperating with Wisconsin Conservation Department, State Parks Division." *Courtesy Wisconsin DNR, Devil's Lake State Park.*

building construction projects. They were the structures that tourists would see and use most often. They were also the ones that CCC higher-ups would see and judge. Even before the building projects began, officials descended on the camp to discuss the plans and inspect the building sites. In one two-month period in early 1936, the camp had its usual visits by Wisconsin Park Authority and inspectors, plus special visits by an NPS regional officer and an NPS geologist who wanted to inspect the shoreline. A Department of Interior mechanic inspector also showed up to make sure the camp tools and equipment were properly inventoried. The parade of inspectors would continue over the life of the CCC program at the park—testimony to the importance of Devil's Lake projects.

Besides the brass from the CCC, others came to the park to observe and study. The University of Wisconsin–Madison regularly scheduled summer field studies at the lake—a tradition that predated the CCC era. University professor G.W. Longenecker had thirty of his landscape architecture students at the lake in the summer of 1941. By that time, all the rustic buildings at the park were completed. Also by that time, Longenecker had established himself as the guiding hand behind the CCC camp at the University Arboretum and its famous prairie restoration project. That summer, the students of Longenecker's class had the opportunity to see everything the NPS had done during the CCC era and how it had impacted the park environment. Additionally, they talked to NPS staff and CCC boys about their mission and how it was fulfilled. It was a well-timed visit, even though the university students didn't realize it at the moment. They would be the last group to see the NPS and CCC in action. Six months later, the camp was closed and the personnel sent home or scattered to other assignments.[60]

Of course, the CCC boys knew about the visits by administrative big shots and scholars from the university, but it is just as likely that they went about their duties and didn't pay much attention to the men with ties and notebooks poking around. Odbert knew state and local officials would be watching the progress of jobs, and he knew they had to be done right. He also knew he needed help. Putting up a building was on a much higher learning plateau for workers than planting trees. Odbert needed knowledgeable LEMs to train the enrollees in the basics of survey engineering, carpentry, masonry and cement work, plumbing, roofing and interior finishing. These were trade skills that required precise calculations. Somehow, it all came together—but it wasn't easy. The payoff for Eugene Odbert was seeing the buildings go up year after year all over the park.

The most anticipated building project was the new bathhouse on the north shore beach. It also happened to be the first large construction project approved for the CCC in the Wisconsin State Parks system. Early in 1936, a frame building that had served as the current bathhouse "had a general untidy appearance which was the cause of considerable adverse criticism from park visitors." Getting rid of that eyesore was the first step in transforming the north shore, but that job was not a reckless demolition. The old structure was "carefully torn down" by the CCC crew in preparation for the new facility. Useable lumber from the old building was stored for future use in construction elsewhere in the park.[61]

In accordance with NPS master plans, the new building going up on the north shoreline was designed to fit with the natural surroundings as closely as possible. Crucial to fulfilling that ideal was the search for construction materials that were native to the Baraboo Hills. At the top of the construction list was attractive building stone. Amazingly, the proper stone for the buildings in the park was not far from the CCC camp. The stone would come mostly from the previously abandoned quartzite works on the south bluff, known locally as the Hopkins Quarry. The quarry had

Enrollees at work inside the bathhouse, 1936. *Courtesy Wisconsin DNR, Devil's Lake State Park.*

been operational for decades prior to the arrival of the CCC boys, with much of the stone harvested for projects far away. Things were about to change. Now, the CCC crews would use the quarry stone for all the big building projects in the park. Lavender quartzite, which had dominated the bluffs surrounding the lake for thousands of years, would now dominate the new structures at Devil's Lake.

The most practical challenge for the young men was to safely remove the stone from the quarry. Next, they used chisels to shape and bring out the brilliance and color hues of the stone. Quartzite is beautiful but also a hard type of tightly compacted sandstone, so considerable work was necessary to shape the pieces after they were taken from the quarry pit. Another gravel pit on the north side of the lake supplied additional blocks of quartzite that were ever so slightly different in color from those taken from the south quarry.

Of course, there was some building material that was not available in the park. In a rare assignment outside the park boundaries, a CCC crew from Devil's Lake was sent to the "Ableman District," about a dozen miles west of the park (near present Rock Springs), to quarry red sandstone for the outdoor terrace floor of the bathhouse. Logs from the surrounding area would provide roof support, while finished lumber from town would be used for doors and window framing. The whole thing would be topped off by cedar shingles brought in from northern Wisconsin.

Stones for park building construction were harvested at more than one site. This one is on the north end of the park. The use of more than one quarry resulted in different color hues that added to the beauty of the rustic-style architecture. *Courtesy Wisconsin DNR, Devil's Lake State Park.*

During the winter of 1935–36, CCC enrollees began work at the quarry preparing a stockpile of building stone to be used in the spring. As difficult and backbreaking as that type of work could be, and perhaps to relieve the boredom of winter at camp, the boys lined up to take on that assignment. Project supervisor Odbert reported that "practically the entire company requested permission to work in the quarry." Despite unusually cold weather that season, the frigid conditions did carry at least one advantage at the job site. Winter made the use of sleds to move stone blocks from the quarry a very practical option. Meanwhile, in the indoor comfort of the camp buildings, other enrollees were working alongside civil engineers to help draft final blueprints for the bathhouse and other shelter buildings in the park.[62]

Long Wisconsin winters certainly had an impact on the crews, as well as on the projects at Devil's Lake. While work adjustments had to be made for bitter cold and the occasional blizzard that kept the men in camp for days, the boys were otherwise prepared for harsh weather. Commanders made sure that each enrollee was equipped with long johns, wool pants, several pairs of wool socks, a sweater, a heavy jacket, gloves and mittens and a hat with flaps that folded down over the ears. If that wasn't enough, enrollees could report to the supply sergeant and make their case for additional clothing. The supply sergeant was also available to replace worn-out or damaged clothing as long as the enrollees turned in the worn items.

Cold weather didn't stop a crew from installing drainpipes for the bathhouse in 1936. Before undertaking such projects, local tradesmen were hired to teach the young men the skills necessary to do a good job. *Courtesy Wisconsin DNR, Devil's Lake State Park.*

Even Odbert and others knew that winter conditions were going to change the work schedule no matter how mild or bitterly cold it got. Odbert reported that the winter of 1935–36 was especially cruel, with conditions among the worst in fifty years. Heavy snow and intense cold in February 1936 slowed down work and kept the men in camp much of that time. Some building tasks such as mortar mixing and concrete work could not be attempted during cold weather. When that happened, the men were assigned different tasks. For example, a selected group of young men received training in the operation of bulldozing equipment for snow removal. Camp officials managed to get Sauk County to loan them a metal blade, which was then attached to one of the camp's big tractors. The equipment was put to good use for snow removal on the road into and out of camp.[63]

The arrival of better weather did not always mean smooth sailing. The spring thaw created mud bog conditions at many of the work sites. Galoshes and gloves were a must for everyone, and at the job site, it was sometimes necessary to create wood plank roads in order to accommodate wheel-barrel traffic that would otherwise sink into the muck. Given such conditions, modern equipment and new machinery were always a welcome sight. A big help on the bathhouse project was the timely arrival of ten new Dodge trucks in the fall of 1936.

A camp Caterpillar with a plow blade on loan from Sauk County, January 1936. Superintendent Odbert reported that snow removal—not project work—was often the most significant part of camp life during their first winter. *Courtesy Wisconsin DNR, Devil's Lake State Park.*

With the spring thaw, construction on the bathhouse began in earnest. Gravel for the building site was trucked in, but large quartzite blocks from the quarry at the south end were put aboard a special rail car and transported to the construction site at the north end via the line running along the east side of the lake. Likewise, the crew collecting flagstone near Rock Springs had access to a rail line that ran from its location directly into the park and very close to the bathhouse site. Smaller blocks of stone, quarried during the winter, were transported by truck to the north side.

Following the tough winter of late 1935, extreme weather of a different kind hit the state just as the bathhouse project was getting cranked up for the 1936 summer construction period. A record-setting heat wave blasted central Wisconsin in July and August. On July 13 at Wisconsin Dells (just a few miles north of Devil's Lake), the mercury hit 114 degrees—the highest temperature ever recorded in Wisconsin. Fifty miles south of the lake in Madison, early July saw six of seven days with temperatures over 100 degrees. On July 13, Madison recorded a temperature of 107—the highest in the city's history. That same day, every weather-reporting station in Wisconsin, except one (on an island in Lake Michigan), recorded a temperature above 100 degrees.

A month before the heat wave struck, Odbert instituted double-shift work, undoubtedly hoping to make up for lost time from the previous winter but

Typical springtime working conditions at a CCC job site at Devil's Lake in 1937. *Courtesy Richard McDavitt.*

also to get the parking project done so visitor traffic could access the lake during the height of the summer tourist season. The first group of men worked from 6:00 a.m. until noon, and the second shift went from noon until 6:00 p.m. Odbert put as many men on the job as the shoreline could safely accommodate. Ultimately, over 85 percent of camp enrollees were working on various north shore projects in the early summer of 1936.

The double schedule played havoc with the cooks back at camp on the south shore. Even during the long sunshine days of June, cooking crews had to roll out of their bunks and fumble around in the early morning twilight in order to have things ready in time for the first set of workers. A total of six meals had to be served during the day, with the first one coming at 5:15 a.m. and the final evening meal at 6:30 p.m. Both meal and work schedules went haywire again when the central Wisconsin heat wave struck. More delays ensued, but both the cook staff and work crews plugged away. By May 1937, the bathhouse building was finally nearing completion.[64]

The north shore bathhouse was an ambitious undertaking, by far the biggest building project in the park. As the first and most visible building, Odbert wanted everything to be perfect. Much of it depended on the LEMs. They stood over the enrollees every step of the way. Often, they were literally standing next to the young teenagers as they placed stones for the building walls. Supervisors and inspectors were at the construction site every day, making sure window and door frames were aligned correctly, helping

A job supervisor (kneeling) instructs enrollees on the placement of building stones in the construction of the bathhouse. *Courtesy Wisconsin DNR, Devil's Lake State Park.*

to choose the proper size quartzite block for a particular placement and teaching the finer points of roofing.

Since construction went on for a year, the bathhouse project lasted longer than some enrollee enlistments. That meant that some boys who had so enthusiastically started the project and developed valuable building skills along the way were discharged from the CCC program and went home before being able to gaze upon the finished structure. More importantly, it also meant that crew foremen and supervisors had to train a whole new group of recruits in the construction trades halfway through the job.

Stone masonry, even using the rustic standards of the NPS, was a more challenging job for enrollees and supervising engineers than it would first appear. At the quarry, enrollees would use picks, chains and winches (but no explosives) to break off and select just the right size boulders. LEMs were standing by to observe safety rules and also help in the selection of the most colorful quartzite. Once the rocks made their way to the job site, they would be individually placed on benches at single workstations. Dozens of CCC boys spent many hours standing at the benches and shaping quartzite blocks using a hammer and chisel. Their work required long hours of standing, sweating and sculpting flat surfaces so the stone could be dropped into a prearranged yet natural-looking slot in the building wall.

Preparing the quartzite boulder before placement in one of the building walls. This unknown enrollee is violating at least two safety rules by not wearing gloves on both hands and going shirtless while working with chipping tools. *Courtesy Wisconsin DNR, Devil's Lake State Park.*

Enrollees were not simply handed tools and released to the job site. At all jobs in the park, safety was a big part of the training. Regular meetings were held at the camp and at the construction site. First aid kits were present at each job site. Tools and other equipment were inspected weekly, and conditions were reported to district headquarters. At Devil's Lake, Odbert hired gruff and crusty William Marquardt as a LEM with the title of "tool keeper," whose sole job was to account for and make sure equipment was properly maintained. It was all part of the safety program. For the stone-chipping boys, safety goggles were required, along with heavy work gloves, as sharp shards of stone flew from the worktable with each blow from the chisel.

While long rectangular blocks were meticulously measured and shaped for use in windowsills and door thresholds, the rustic style allowed for deliberate imperfections elsewhere. The color nuances of the rock used in construction at the park were both a pleasant coincidence and an opportunity for creative expression. In the rustic scheme of things, native stones of different color

The north shore bathhouse nears completion in late 1936. The cedar logs stacked against the tree will join others in place to form the palisade for the west end open-air dressing area. *Courtesy Richard McDavitt.*

hues were considered quite proper and attractive. Shades of medium brown, gray and especially the distinctive pink and deep lavender of the quartzite at Devil's Lake are all present in the building walls of structures put up by the CCC. These shades of rock color caused by exposure, water, different quarry locations and eons of inclement weathering gave the buildings a distinctive yet natural appearance—just what the National Park Service was looking for. Degrees of color variations in the rock were just a passing thought to the men who were at work on the building scaffolding each day. The boys were intent on getting the job done and doing it right. Despite having supervisors and work foremen watching their every move, there is evidence that the boys still enjoyed what they were doing and learned from the experience. The camp newspaper reported that the stone workers "really went to town" on the bathhouse project, and the carpentry crew put the huge log roof beams into place "without a hitch." It was agreed that "the men on these crews admit they learned at least something every day and a great deal more than they ever knew before about construction."[65]

Enrollees could be rightly proud of the job they had done. The bathhouse was a completely modern yet rustic-looking facility. The finished structure had two wings off a central interior meeting area—the east side reserved for women and the west side for men. Toilets, shower facilities and private dressing booths were of course available on each side. Also, each wing had an enclosed yet open-air (for sanitation reasons) section for dressing. The

Bathhouse construction, 1936. On a crisp November day, crews pour the concrete foundation for the flagstone terrace. This photo is by NPS project superintendent Eugene Odbert and was part of a series intended to document each phase of the construction. This part of the building faces the lake. *Courtesy Wisconsin DNR, Devil's Lake State Park.*

area was screened from public view by a vertical palisade of heavy logs built on a quartzite base. The central part of the building consisted of a common area, where attendants greeted bathers and issued baskets for personal belongings, as well as brass keys for the limited locker spaces available. Just outside, a small native flagstone patio area faced the lake.

The building experience learned from the bathhouse project was incorporated into other building projects in the park, despite enrollment turnover with new recruits coming on. Other north shore projects in the early years included development of camping and picnic grounds, a sewer and water system, stone culverts (using native quartzite of course), a parking area and a water storage facility. The water storage project caught the attention of the camp inspector in 1937. Located at the highest point in the north campground, the thirty-thousand-gallon-capacity reservoir was being built below ground to conform to NPS standards of visually integrating projects into the landscape. Even though it was half finished at the time, the CCC district inspector characterized the job as "impressive."

Planned by the NPS and developed by the CCC, Northern Lights campground continues to serve campers. From a historical perspective, the layout of the campsites is less important than the structures that remain from

The carpentry crew at work framing a small bathhouse in the Northern Lights campground. The adjoining wooden shed was temporary and likely used for equipment storage. *Courtesy Wisconsin DNR, Devil's Lake State Park.*

the 1930s. The campground still contains two small bathhouses and a stone shelter that are the work of CCC quartzite masons. As with the lakeside buildings, these hidden architectural gems display the rustic style, but moreover are a testament to the careful yet natural-looking construction efforts of a team of young men learning a trade for the first time and getting it right.

One of the last big construction projects was the park administration building on the north shore built during the 1939–40 season. The building design was the work of architect Bernard H. Knobla. He was already well known among NPS and Wisconsin park officials for a number of projects, including his rustic design buildings at Copper Falls and Rib Mountain State Parks, plus the earlier bathhouse project at Devil's Lake. He also had a hand in the master plan project for the park at St. Croix Falls. No architect was more connected to the Wisconsin state park system during the CCC era than Knobla.

A new road alignment on the north shore was directly related to the placement of the new administration building. Officials planning the new project were alarmed by the increased traffic in the area. Visitors were using an old road to motor onto the beach at the north end. Construction of the new building provided the excuse needed to save the north beach area from the ever-growing flood of automobiles. The old road was "obliterated" in favor of creating a new road running east–west in front of the north entrance to the yet-to-be-built administration building. The road change saved the shoreline by preventing vehicles from being driven to the beaches at the north end. The new alignment instead led visitors to the new parking lot or the wooded camping areas away from the lake.[66] It was an environmental protection move taken during a time when many people believed the lake could naturally recover from almost anything inflicted by summer tourists.

The administration facility constructed by the CCC boys still serves as the park headquarters in the twenty-first century and is the first CCC building that park visitors see when they drive down to the flatland at the northern end of the lake. Its placement by architect Knobla, supervisor Odbert and other park officials away from the Chateau and bathhouse served to visually open up the north shore and funnel cars to designated parking areas, leaving pedestrians and swimmers to fully enjoy the sandy shoreline and nearby picnic areas free from haphazard vehicle encroachment.

Once again using quartzite from the area, the administration facility became the final piece of CCC building construction in the park. Of course, it was designed to blend nicely with the earlier CCC structures. But while all the buildings were in the rustic style, the discerning eye can notice the different type of workmanship found in the details of the bathhouse of 1937 compared with the administration building of 1939–40. Both buildings are on the north shore and just a short distance from each other. Yet different

The completed north parking lot is an excellent example of how CCC projects at the park could be immediately seen and used by the public. The lot continues to be the closest auto access to the north beach. *Courtesy Wisconsin DNR, Devil's Lake State Park.*

Getting the Job Done

Landscaping on the nearly completed park administration building in 1940. The structure was the last big building project undertaken in the park by the CCC. Note the unfinished roof. The Chateau and East Bluff can be seen in the background. *Courtesy Wisconsin DNR, Devil's Lake State Park.*

hues of rock color and degrees of attention to the details of mortar work are the two most noticeable changes for anyone who takes a nose-to-the-stone tour around each building. All of the stone structures in the park seem to have their own special characteristics, despite having common building materials. While the buildings are the most obvious and impressive examples of CCC craftsmanship and accomplishments, much more work by enrollees was done out of sight of most tourists yet still was of great benefit to many of them.

Hiking is a big part of the Devil's Lake experience. To fully understand the geology and beauty of the park, one must take a walk. Balanced Rock, Devil's Doorway, Elephant Rock, Cleopatra's Needle and many other geologic oddities can be viewed only by walking away from the lake. A climb to the bluffs overlooking the water was an exhausting yet awesome sightseeing adventure. The CCC boys made the trip many times during the 1930s. Theirs was mostly a route to work, but like the winter climbing group intent on getting a snowy picture of the camp, they occasionally made the trip just for the fun of it.

State park personnel had long known the network of trails was a great teaching environment and enlisted the CCC in publicizing its wonders. Enrollee Bruce Budde recalls leading a group of schoolchildren on a hike in 1941 that started at the trail across from the camp, went up to the top of the bluff and then down the other side and ended at the Chateau. Having built and maintained much of the popular trails in the park over the years, it was fitting that the young enrollees would get a chance to talk to and instruct visitors on what they built and what it meant.[67]

Considering years of modern maintenance and repair, it is sometimes difficult to identify specific areas of CCC trail improvement today, but the CCCers were active in trail construction almost every year of camp operation. It was exhausting and labor-intensive work. In keeping with NPS guidelines and approval by the State of Wisconsin, trail work in the park using heavy machinery or motorized equipment was prohibited. It was felt that roaring motors would not only be a distraction to visitors seeking wilderness solitude, but also the use of such equipment and its movement up and down the trails would unnecessarily tear up the nearby ground vegetation, create gullies, knock down small trees, disturb wildlife and contribute to possible worker injuries.

The way it usually worked was that a crew of about six would be assigned a section of trail. A LEM went along at first to make sure proper safety procedures were followed. Enrollees were allowed to use winches, steel leverage rods and chains to get the job done, but sometimes the simplest thing to do was to pick up a loose boulder and toss it aside. For movement

Enrollees working on the Balanced Rock Trail on the steep face of the East Bluff. No gas-powered or electric machinery was used on trail construction. Two- or four-man hand boxes (on the ground in the center of photo) were used to lift unwieldy stones. *Courtesy Wisconsin DNR, Devil's Lake State Park.*

of bigger rocks, they constructed wooden boxes with handles at each end, making it possible for two or four men to lift and carry.

The Balanced Rock Trail is a good place to see remnants of CCC work. Beginning near the southeast shore, it switch-backed up the south face of the bluff, first through a small stand of timber and then sharply up through the pink quartzite talus field with its enormous boulders. The CCC boys had to climb up and down every day to get to their work station. Each day, they worked their way a little higher, winching large rocks aside to make a path. In the course of their work, the boys looked around the talus debris to find other stones suitable in size and shape to be used as part of the trail. Chipping was sometimes necessary to create a flat surface before a stone could be placed. They wielded huge boulders of quartzite, requiring lifting by two or more men, and carefully placed them on the trail, making sure they were aligned with the previous stones so hikers could more easily step up. Each day, the same process of climbing, lifting and placing was repeated. Nearly the entire length of the Balance Rock Trail is a handmade stone stairway rising five hundred feet from the lakeshore.

The present-day foot trail leading directly from the old CCC campsite and up the south face of the East Bluff is also the work of Company 2669. In later years, it was appropriately called the CCC Trail. Begun in the summer of 1939 and finished the following year, the trail pushed up and over the same talus field of quartzite that the Balanced Rock Trail had conquered, once again using native stone to create steps to the top of the bluff and once again switch-backing upward using the natural features of the slope to their best advantage. Project superintendent Odbert reported that after topping out, the trail crew continued construction westward along the edge of the bluff as far as Devil's Doorway.

Clarence Guetzkow worked on the CCC Trail during its later stages, when the young men were working far up on the talus slope. He still remembers how he and the crew could look directly down on the camp buildings, but Clarence made a point of not getting too close a look. "I learned to stay away from the edge and be careful," he said. "It was long way down. But one CCC fellow broke his arm when he fell off the trail and onto the big boulders up there."

Just as the bathhouse and other buildings in the park corresponded to NPS construction guidelines, so too did the trail crews adhere to the rustic standards. Both the Balanced Rock and CCC trails are excellent examples of blending construction with the natural surroundings. Both trails navigate through the south talus slopes with barely a noticeable disturbance to

A view of the southern end of Devil's Lake from near the crest of the East Bluff in 1937. Enrollees building what is now called the CCC Trail would have enjoyed this view as they worked their way up the cliff side. *Courtesy Richard McDavitt.*

the surrounding tumble-down rock—only the stone steps hint at human interference. The steps themselves are universally, and by necessity, uneven in width and height from one to the next and in places are often only wide enough for one person at a time to pass.

The NPS master plan suggested stone placement without mortar, although some segments were cemented in later years by state park workers as a safety measure. The CCC boys built no handrails, nor did they install ropes lines or put in trailside benches. They planted no shade trees as a respite for hikers. The primitive trail construction features were deliberate in an effort to create a minimal impact on the land and also to make an exhilarating and self-rewarding experience for the hiker. Viewing the trail from afar is the best measure of its rustic success. A person standing on the southeast shore of the lake looking directly at the south talus rock field a few hundred feet away will not see a trail—only a tumbled mass of boulders frozen in place on the cliff side.

The East Bluff Trail, completed in 1941, was one of the last big projects before the camp closed. Most of the trail runs across the top of the East Bluff and therefore was longer but much less rocky and steep than the south side trails. The bluff was pleasantly wooded most of the way to the top, with shady oaks replacing the open area and scattered white pines of the talus slopes below. It was still necessary to carry and place stone steps in certain places, but the quiet, cool canopy forest made trail construction much more enjoyable.[68]

100

A rubble-filled section of the Devil's Lake hillside prior to trail development. The wooden box in the foreground was used to remove large boulders and constituted the first step in trail restoration. *Courtesy Wisconsin DNR, Devil's Lake State Park.*

Another assignment that got a lot of attention (but little glamour) during the CCC days was the adventure of the blister rust crew. Anyone assigned to that crew would be guaranteed a day of bent-over, muscle-aching work. It was the most basic of manual labor, all in an effort to interrupt the cycle of tree disease. White pine blister rust is caused by a fungus that can produce "cankers" in the main tree stem of white pines, resulting in tree death. However, the fungus does not transfer directly from tree to tree. Instead, it needs an "alternative host," such as currant or gooseberry bushes, to spread the disease. If these hosts can be removed, then the blister rust cannot be transferred to another tree. Therefore, a continuing project goal was for the CCC boys to get rid of the gooseberry plants in the park. The job required workers to walk through an area, bend over and physically cut or otherwise uproot the bush. No chemical applications were used in the process. It was

A completed section of trail after CCC restoration. Compare to the photo on the previous page. *Courtesy Wisconsin DNR, Devil's Lake State Park.*

a monumental task and seemed to record more injuries (though minor) than trail or building construction work.

Some areas of the park were easily accessible and reasonably level walking for the blister rust crews. Numerous other places involved steep grades and working up the bluffs on three sides of the lake. Even for young men, it was back-aching and dangerous work. The camp paper reported, "This is perhaps the only job with dangerous hazards, because one slip may mean serious injury. However, the boys have a very good record and have had very few accidents." As they worked their way up the slopes, the enrollees also knew that rattlesnakes made their home in the bluffs surrounding the lake. To help generate enthusiasm for the job in the face of those dangers, one foreman in 1936 sponsored a contest between crews, with a camp party for the crew that missed the fewest gooseberry plants.[69]

Of course, enthusiasm for the work among the enrollees ebbed and flowed depending on the jobs involved and often the mood of the person when he awoke that morning. That is why supervisors liked to assign the men to a variety of different tasks over the length of their enrollment periods. The rotation kept the men fresh and also exposed them to different trade skills. Undoubtedly, there was some grumbling at times, but the young men knew they were there to learn, and in general many saw their assignments as a personal challenge rather than as a distasteful duty.

One day, Devil's Lake enrollee Walter Lahl drew the assignment of planting sapling trees. The eighteen-year-old got right to work and finished with his allotted trees faster than his companions. Walter didn't do it all himself, but

Command staff and cooks from a detail of the 1937 Devil's Lake official CCC panoramic photograph. Shown in the photo are Eugene Odbert (seated third from right), W.R. Winkelmeyer (seated third from left) and Bob Karow (back row, center, wearing necktie). *Courtesy Richard McDavitt.*

he recalled, "One day we planted six hundred trees." Another member of the crew said it was impossible to finish that job in a short amount of time. Wally must have planted two trees in one hole, he said. Wally relished an investigation. When the supervisor checked the field, he found that Wally's work was properly done. He was simply a young and energetic worker with a strong back. About that job, Wally later said, "I got to work and kept on going. I didn't stop to smoke a cigarette or talk to anyone. I just wanted to get the job done."[70] Wally never mentioned if his speed at tree planting was because of his enthusiasm for outdoor conservation work or his desire to quickly complete an assignment.

While most enrollees were outdoors working on projects during the day, a small contingent of CCC boys was stationed at camp as support personnel. For example, if an enrollee was proficient on a typewriter (or willing to learn), he was often recruited by the commanding officer to help with clerical duties in the camp office. Two or three such people were necessary to keep up with the paperwork. Of course, the all-important kitchen staff included four or five cooks plus a mess sergeant and a small number of KP draftees. The camp also had a carpentry/metals workshop, plus a vehicle maintenance garage.

It was a different kind of life working inside the camp. At Devil's Lake in 1940, enrollee Bruce Budde was part of the seven-man crew working in the carpentry shop. The crew got ready for work each day and reported to the parade ground like the others did for work assignments. But instead of climbing onto trucks and leaving camp for the work site, the carpentry boys would head to the carpentry building in the southwest corner of the camp. After getting their assignments for the day, they could work at their own pace with little supervision. "I liked the work I was doing…the work was steady but not hard, and the time went by fast," Budde recalled. Even if the work was "not hard," it was still essential to the operation and success of the camp projects. "We made picnic tables and did sign engraving and painting," said Budde.

I remember the park service wanted to maintain a "rustic" look to its highway signs and I would carve them the way they wanted. We also made cross-arms for telephone poles and bolted them on to the larger pole. Another thing we produced in the shop was circular concrete weights [slabs] that were used to hold down campground grilles. At other times we were asked to fix screens and windows and do some general maintenance around camp.

Perhaps the nicest benefit from working in the camp was winter duty. While most of the men were outdoors in the cold and snow dressed in protective

The garage area. Besides vehicle storage, this area also served as a repair station, woodworking area and tool storage facility. Photo by LEM foreman Marven Hartman, circa 1938. *Courtesy Wisconsin DNR, Devil's Lake State Park.*

layers of clothing, Bruce Budde and his carpentry crew worked in heated comfort and away from the prying eyes of the technical services foremen.[71]

Whether working indoors or out, there were situations when the job called for immediate action in which the regular routine of the day would take a backseat to more pressing matters. Fire was one of those situations. All enrollees received training in fire suppression, and many of them got a chance to use it under real conditions, whether that was actual firefighting, building firebreak roads or trails or serving as lookouts. Such duty did not always take place around the camp. Regional CCC officials routinely called on camps from far and wide to help with a fire somewhere in the state. For example, within weeks of setting up the new camp at Devil's Lake, fifty men were off to the CCC camp at Rib Mountain in central Wisconsin.

Fire also hit close to home for the boys at Devil's Lake. The loveliness of the woods that cover the Baraboo Hills and cradle the lake, providing a shady respite from a hot summer day, can easily be destroyed in short order during a particularly dry fire season. On May 30, 1936, a fire erupted on the East Bluff near Balance Rock, not far from the CCC camp. The entire company of over one hundred men turned out to battle the four-acre blaze. The first step in getting to the fire meant climbing up the dreaded talus slope of quartzite blocks. While brought under control in a single day, mop-up operations took three additional days to make sure the embers did not get a fresh start. Tourist and

Crews on their way out of camp to fight a forest fire, late summer 1936. Project superintendent Eugene Odbert is seen second from right. *Courtesy Wisconsin DNR, Devil's Lake State Park.*

townspeople at the park had front row seats from the lake and were eyewitnesses to the effectiveness of the CCC boys and their fire suppression skills.

Four acres is a small fire by most standards, but things were different at this park. The East Bluff fire could have been a disaster. These were not the empty and remote forests of the American West. This fire was in a popular state park, with hundreds of tourists and novice hikers scattered throughout the dense woods. Fleeing a fire in which the hiker can only see smoke from ground to treetop and not the flame is an especially dangerous situation. Determining directions can be confusing, and it's possible that people fleeing an area could instead be running toward the flames. Panic can be quickly substituted for logic, especially if families with small children are on the trail. Knowing this, measures were taken to give firefighters more time to head off a potentially big blaze. A detail of CCC boys was assigned to patrol the bluffs, scouting for fire and warning hikers about the danger of smoking in the woods. It was a reasonable attempt to buy time if a fire was discovered and an opportunity to promote fire prevention if no fire was active. Not every hiker could be protected in the park, but the CCC commanders figured this small measure would at least boost awareness. To enrollees who thought hiking through the woods, talking to tourists and watching the skyline sounded wonderful, the camp newspaper warned, "This work was not as easy as it might seem. Not many men would climb the bluffs sometimes three and four times a day and every day of the week."[72]

7

ART MCDAVITT'S LONG ROAD
TO DEVIL'S LAKE

Enrollee Art McDavitt was present at Devil's Lake for many of the big projects. The important bathhouse construction job was in full swing, and the underground reservoir work was just getting started. Inspectors and foremen were everywhere, checking every little detail of the construction. Art was used to it all by now. That's because he was not a rookie when he arrived at SP-12. He was a CCC veteran who had already been through the adventure of a lifetime. Yet what happened to Art McDavitt was not unlike the experiences of many seasoned enrollees.

After the creation of Company 2669 from elements of Company 2615 at Milwaukee, there was a turnover of enrollees at Devil's Lake every few months as enlistments expired. The number of men leaving each time fluctuated from just a few to over fifty at one time. The larger number represented over one-third of the company strength. A few young men who were at Devil's Lake reenlisted after six months and continued to serve at the park for several enrollment periods, but such an extended stay beyond two years was rare and technically against organization rules. For many, the young men served one enlistment and went home. Others heard of jobs back home and got permission to leave early, and still others requested transfers to follow friends and adventures at other camps. Art McDavitt was one of the latter. With multiple enlistments under his belt, Art was among a small corps of experienced CCC men who showed up at Devil's Lake to take the place of other enlisted leaders who had moved on.

McDavitt was born and raised in Monticello, Illinois. Located in the flat farm country downstate, Monticello was one among countless, and seemingly

Art McDavitt. By the time he arrived at Devil's Lake, McDavitt was a seasoned enrollee, having served with CCC companies in Illinois and Idaho. *Courtesy Richard McDavitt.*

identical, small towns with a railroad siding connecting it to the farm markets of the Midwest. But Art was not a farm boy and did not come from a railroad family. His parents lived in town and ran a restaurant. When hard times hit Monticello, Arthur looked for a way to help his family and at the same time help himself—but it wasn't going to happen in his hometown.

Word of what the CCC was all about, and its early successes, made its way to southern Illinois, and after a year of hearing about it, Art knew that he had to give it a try. In August 1934, his two-week training regimen began not far from home at Jefferson Barrack in St. Louis. By Labor Day, he was off to his first assignment—a brand-new company (1698) at a brand-new camp. In keeping with the tradition of staying close to home, his new assignment took him to Macomb, in western Illinois. Located a mile south of town, the camp was a Soil Conservation Service (SCS) unit dedicated to erosion control and restoring the tired land by applying the newest soil-saving techniques. McDavitt and his friends didn't mind the work; they got along fine and imagined themselves on a grand adventure. After six months, they reenlisted and spent a comfortable year at the Macomb camp. But the good times, familiar surroundings and weekend passes home did not last.

The dilemma for CCC administrators in Washington was that the sparsely populated West was where the greatest opportunity for forest conservation existed, but enrollment numbers from the West did not keep up with the project needs of the western states. Therefore, to get men to the critical areas of need meant taking units from the more heavily populated East and moving them to the sparsely populated areas of the Rocky Mountain West. At the beginning of a new year, Art McDavitt and his Illinois company got the shocking call to report to Camp Peone in the remote panhandle country of northern Idaho. The news generated confused glances between enrollees. They had never heard of the place. Even looking at a road map didn't help. There was no town of Peone. Late-night discussions in the comfortable barracks of Camp Macomb went back and forth. To some, it didn't matter—it was just someplace different. After all, it was just one more opportunity to experience new things. So on a cold January day in 1936, the boys boarded a train in Macomb and headed west.

Camp Peone (named after a locally famous Indian chief) was half a mile east of Worley, Idaho, on the Coeur d'Alene Indian Reservation. It was Wild West remote by anyone's standards. The closest big city was thirty-seven miles away across the state line in Spokane, Washington. The camp newspaper's first issue from Peone noted that, after disembarking from the train and looking around, their first impression of their new world was that it was "a little quiet out here." To drive home the point, the paper also had a disquieting message from G.H. Dyer, the mayor of Worley: "We realize that our village, being small, affords very little entertainment and amusement compared to larger places."

Art McDavitt's barracks buddies at Peone, Idaho. Enrollees everywhere, including Devil's Lake, spent a lot of free time lounging in their quarters. Besides conversation, reading and card playing were the most popular pastimes. *Courtesy Richard McDavitt.*

Camp Peone was a SCS camp like Macomb, so some of the work assignments were very much like their previous CCC jobs in the Midwest. This new area in which soil conservation efforts would be directed also included cultivated lands for field peas and, of course, Idaho's famous potatoes. As part of the work, Art's company built several rock and log check dams across gullies for erosion control. They also dug trenches for terracing on the hillsides of the mountains surrounding Worley as part of a runoff control project. All the while, Art gained valuable work experience at a variety of jobs and set himself up for a leadership role at his Devil's Lake assignment.

Like the Devil's Lake boys, work was not the most important thing in Art's life. Part of the appeal for Art and the other CCC boys were the new adventures that lay just around the corner. The northern Rockies were new to everyone in the company, so they meant to explore them at any opportunity. The boys got help from a sympathetic camp commander, who was generous with extended leaves to see the country. In the nine months that Art spent at the Idaho camp, he managed to make a grand tour of the region. First, there was Spokane, and then it was on to the impressive work site for Grand Coulee Dam, the largest construction project then underway in the United States. He made it to the Pacific Coast and the mouth of the mighty Columbia River at Astoria, Oregon. It was there that Lewis and Clark first glimpsed the Pacific Ocean 130 years before. A final fling later took him to the famous rodeo roundup in Pendleton, Oregon. He was careful to take lots of photographs; folks would never believe it back in Monticello.

In the meantime, enlistments expired, and men moved on. The boys from rural Illinois with whom Art joined up were mostly gone now. But Art enjoyed the memories, friendships and even some of the work. He wanted to find a reason to stay. Besides, times were still tough, and what was waiting back home? Authorizations for Art to transfer to Company 2669 at Devil's Lake and continue his CCC service well past his normal discharge date somehow sailed through the bureaucracy. By November 1936, he was reporting to Devil's Lake State Park, Wisconsin, for an experience unlike anything he had seen before.

The bathhouse project was progressing nicely, and the park was abuzz with construction activity, but as a "rookie," Art's first assignment involved loading gravel for use at the building site. However, it wasn't long before camp officials found out about his previous service and work experience. Camp commanders and project foremen were always looking for boys like Art—boys who knew the camp routine and could properly direct the men when no other authority figures were present. He was quickly promoted to

On the job during the early stages of the reservoir project. Enrollees used a "plank highway" to more easily remove dirt from a foundation pit. *Courtesy Richard McDavitt.*

one of the camp leadership positions, joining longtime Devil's Lake veterans Robert Karow, J.E. Brack and Ralph Clinton.

Art didn't have a lot to do with the bathhouse construction, but he did get to work on another big project: the underground water reservoir system in the campground. Like his initial gravel pit duty, the reservoir project was a lot of pick and shovel work, but there was always time to stop and take a few pictures. Of course, in the CCC there was always a lot of pick and shovel work, but some kinds of work were more interesting than others.

One of Art's better assignments was with the tree transplanting crew. This kind of work did not deal with tree saplings that could be held in the palm of one's hand. The bigger trees the boys took on needed special attention and the help of heavy equipment. First, a crew of four to six men was required to dig around the root system of a young tree. Too big to simply pull out of the ground by hand, a bulldozer was needed to come in and tilt the tree so the root system could be wrapped in burlap. Then, chains could be attached underneath the bundle, and it would be ready for transport. Next, the heavy equipment would drag it to a holding area. As more transplants were added to the storage area, the place began to look like a field of upside-down mushrooms. When the weather was favorable, the trees would be hauled one by one to their new location, and crews would again dig a hole. It wasn't rocket science, but some knowledge of tree development and root system stress was necessary in order to do the job correctly. Art learned, and filed away this forestry experience.

The tree transplanting crew. *Courtesy Wisconsin DNR, Devil's Lake State Park.*

In the meantime, Art's passionate hobby of photography was making him famous around camp. He kept a scrapbook photo album that he had started at Jefferson Barracks when he first joined and took with him to Macomb and, later, Idaho. Now he was all over Devil's Lake taking pictures of enrollees at work and around camp. Wherever Art's job assignment took him, his camera went with him. Before he left in 1937, many of his friends who appeared in the photo album signed his scrapbook. Hometown addresses written in the margins, plus photographic images of barracks buddies from his lake duty, are testament to the friends he made. They signed in much the same way high school graduates sign yearbooks, reminding themselves of the good times and shared experiences and yet knowing they may never see one another again.

When Art was discharged from the CCC in 1937, he began looking for work that would match the skills he picked up while he was away from home. He started with a job at the Davey Tree Company back in his hometown of Monticello. Undoubtedly, his recent CCC background in tree transplanting had something to do with his hiring. It was the kind of first step that President Roosevelt had intended for all young men when the CCC program began. Roosevelt's dream carried Art McDavitt from tree planting and camp leader at Devil's Lake to a successful career and comfortable life as a member of America's greatest generation. In a larger sense, Art McDavitt became one of Franklin Roosevelt's New Deal success stories even though the two had never met.[73]

8

THE CAMP NEWSPAPER

The lifeblood of camp news, projects, jokes and gossip was the camp newspaper. Across America, almost every CCC camp tried to put together a paper. National administrators, camp commanders and education advisors all encouraged it, but ultimately it was an effort generated and run by the enrollees themselves. They picked an editor, artist, reporters, typists and others needed to publish a monthly catchall of camp news. It was immensely popular among the enrollees. While the government put out reams of dry reports on CCC activity and inventory, it was the camp newspaper that focused on the human side of life in the camps. Perhaps more than anything else, the true nature of what the CCC was all about can be found by reading the camp newspapers.

The national CCC organization had its own newspaper called *Happy Days*. It was a headquarters paper that printed general CCC news and national perspective on the program. But more importantly, *Happy Days* sought to be an example for individual, enrollee-driven camp news. Through its pages, the paper advised other camps in all states to start their own newspapers. Yet the remote individual camps faced inherent production challenges. They did not have the printing capabilities that a regular newspaper possessed. Therefore, the easiest method for most camps (including Devil's Lake for a time) was to type their stories on a typewriter using mimeograph paper. From there, it was easy to run off as many copies as they needed on a small machine. The downside was that even though the process was quick and easy for text, it was not possible to reprint photographs or other illustrations. Alas, as a final resort, it was feasible to have talented enrollees draw on the mimeograph paper and

The camp newspaper cover from November 1936 shows the typical hand-drawn style that was developed by an enrollee artist. The cover subject, Balance Rock, was a well-known landmark high on the south face of the East Bluff with a view of the lake. *Courtesy Center for Research Libraries, Chicago.*

run off a copy from that. All copies would then be stapled or folded together for distribution to the men at camp. In time, it was possible to upgrade the look of the paper by sending the newspaper copy to a professional printer.[74]

Another factor that had an impact on the look of the paper were the men themselves. Putting together a camp paper was a voluntary effort by the enrollees. They were still responsible for their regular camp duties, so that influenced the amount of time they could spend improving the look of the paper. Most had no training in journalism, although classes were offered at many of the camps. The education advisor often became the paper's editorial adviser as well, but it was up to the men to make the paper a reality. A staff of about eight enrollees was necessary to put out a monthly issue; many boys tried it for a while and handed off the job to someone else at camp. However, if there was at least one eager editor at camp, he could take the lead in pushing others to produce a quality product.

A key element of the paper was the name. Most often chosen by the enrollees, it was meant to be catchy and unique to their camp location. Shortly after arriving at Devil's Lake, some of the men held small group discussions in the tents about a paper and what it should be called. Trial balloons were floated. Finally, a decision was made. It would be called *Devil's Lake Bluff*. The title was certainly appropriate for the park and the camp founded in the shadows of the East Bluff. As company enrollments expired and new recruits came on, the paper was passed to new enrollee management. During one of those transitions in 1938, the paper was temporarily suspended but quickly brought back as *Devil's Mutterings*. During 1940–41, the camp paper disappeared once again, thankfully to be resurrected for the farewell issue of October 1941.

The cover of the Devil's Lake paper in the early days was most often a pencil drawing of a rock formation or special event held at camp. More visually sophisticated options for the cover were out of the question, mostly because equipment was simply not available at the camp to duplicate photographs. Thus, it was important to find a decent artist around camp who could add some interest to the paper with a drawing. Someone with at least a small measure of talent was always found, and occasionally a gem of an artist was discovered. In any case, the newspaper staff at camp made do, and as enrollees came and went, the quality of the art fluctuated too. Nobody seemed to mind.

Who was the true audience for the camp paper? Some say the reason the paper existed was to let the folks back home know what was going on at the camp. It is certainly true that many papers were folded in such a way as to make it possible to address the outside and affix a stamp. Others simply noted that the paper was intended to inform individual enrollees about what was going on in camp while they were on the job with a work crew. Since the editorial staff of each of the camp papers was made up of individual enrollees with individual objectives, it is hard to determine what is true. However, a cover-to-cover reading of the Devil's Lake newspaper suggests that it was meant to keep the boys up to date about jobs going on elsewhere in the park while naming names as a way to give special recognition to individual effort.

For example, the paper of March 31, 1937, said, "The work that Hartman's crew did in transplanting the trees on the north end makes the area look much better. The work of digging them out of the woods was done by Bokina's Rookies." Mundane as such news seems today, it was a big part of enrollees' life at the camp, and they looked forward to seeing their work accomplishments show up in print. Snippets of work information were combined with other project activity in the park, much of it dealing with work that some enrollees knew only through bits of incomplete information picked up in the barracks. With half a dozen projects going at the same time, it was not unusual, even through barracks gossip, for the boys to lose track of what was going on beyond their own job assignments.

In 1938, an unnamed enrollee reporter for *Devil's Mutterings* captured in one short column the kind of information other young men at the camp

Tasks as simple as loading gravel into a truck would go unnoticed and unrewarded were it not for an occasional mention in the camp newspaper. *Courtesy Wisconsin DNR, Devil's Lake State Park.*

really wanted to know. The reporter got up one weekday morning and began a tour of the work sites at the park:

> *We started our morning rounds…by stopping at the shelter house. Here we find approximately 14 men busy slipping the barks off logs and others plainning* [sic] *them…This all pertains to the making of bench tables. Leaving the shelter house and going to the north end…we find Mr. Gehrmann's crew busy with picks and shovels removing the old black-top road. He* [also] *has five men building rock banisters to the culverts which were made last fall by Mr. Carlson's crew…We now go to Mr. Powell's crew where we find approximately 40 men leveling out a large area for the aid of the sewage system…The pouring of the cement into the forms…will be done this week.* [75]

For a time, Devil's Lake published a newspaper edition twice a month. Later, the paper scaled back to a more manageable once a month. But in almost every issue, there was a message from the commanding officer, usually passing along words of encouragement or announcing new events around camp. Sometimes the paper would include a brief company history for the new recruits. It was routine for each issue to include a full page devoted to camp sports. It was also a matter of routine for the education advisor to write a brief column outlining new class offerings.

Outstanding field trips were often scheduled as part of the camp education classes, but they cannot be found in official documents. Many of the trips were quite popular with the men, perhaps as much to relieve the day-to-day doldrums as to educate. Most often, the only mention of them is a column in the camp paper. Without this kind of notice in the paper, a special segment of life in the CCC would be lost to history forever. For example, in late 1936, there were trips by the Devil's Lake enrollees to the state experimental farm at Poynette; then another to the electric power plant on the Wisconsin River at Sauk City. Later, the camp geology class made the short trip to beautiful Parfrey's Glen in the woods east of the lake. None of these educational outings is mentioned in official reports.

In early 1937, education advisor William Winkelmeyer organized perhaps the most popular trip in the company's history. Over one third of SP-12 enrollees (including a contingent from the camp conservation class) went to Madison to visit the Forest Products Lab of the U.S. Forest Service. Established in 1910, the lab was the science center of the nation for tree research. Wood samples from all over the country were sent here to determine wood fiber strength, examine fire-damaged logs and conduct experiments that would have an impact on everything from preservatives for railroad ties to determining the best wood material for building homes. Winkelmeyer's purpose, of course, was to make a connection for the men between the kind of forestry and conservation work they were doing at the park and the kind of forest management and wood science that was going on at the lab.

If wood science was all that was going to happen on the field trip, Winkelmeyer's tour would not have been the success that it was. The boys knew there were going to be some extra stops on this trip. A guided tour of the magnificent Wisconsin state capitol building, with inevitable comparisons to the U.S. Capitol, was one of those extra stops. Next, there was dinner at Henry Vilas Park, where the boys got a look at the city's collection of zoo animals. The trip ended with a visit to the Wisconsin Memorial Library and its collection of Indian relics. The low-keyed reporter for the paper characterized the trip as a successful demonstration of "visual education."

It was a universal fact that over the six months or longer tour of duty in the CCC, many enrollees at camps across the country picked up a nickname from others in the barracks. Oftentimes, the name was passed around for a while and then forgotten. Sometimes, only a few men knew and used the nickname as part of a continuing "inside" joke. Such labeling occurred at Devil's Lake but with an added twist. Instead of ignoring the special names, the camp paper of Company 2669 seized upon the opportunity to mention a nickname whenever a man's name appeared in print. Nicknames were substituted for first names so often that it is sometimes impossible to identify a man's given name. The practice became a tradition that spanned the six-year run of newspaper publishing at Devil's Lake no matter what enrollee editor was in charge.

Hardly any of the enrollee nicknames were mean-spirited. Most often, the nickname assigned to the enrollee had something to do with the man's job, physical characteristics or special talent. For example, there was sports star Edwin "Slug" Johnson. His name was mentioned often in the paper, and a less-than-careful reader might think the nickname to be especially disparaging. However, the term used was shorthand for "slugger," since Mr. Johnson was one of the camp's best baseball players. "Joe Louis" Arnoldini was known for his interest in boxing. Irv "Butch" Johnson (no relation to Edwin) was the man the rest of the enrollees went to for a haircut. J.E. "Tiny" Brack was the overweight barracks leader. Tall and stocky, there was mess steward "Big Bob" Karow. Stories of how "Popeye" Hufford and "Ground Hog" Wilson got their nicknames are unfortunately not offered. Through it

The enrollee on the left wears a custom-made sweatshirt with his camp nickname, "Slim," on the front. The rest of the shirt reads, "Co 2669 CCC, Devil's Lake." *Courtesy Wisconsin DNR, Devil's Lake State Park.*

all, the writers and editors of the camp newspaper wisely avoided attaching or publishing the nicknames of camp commanders or project foremen. Those were left to informally circulate among the late-night card games in the barracks.

Incidents of humor and acts of heroism, however small, never made it into the official reports, but they made it into the *Devil's Lake Bluff*. Kitchen steward A.J. Bowens became the "Hero of the Month" in the March 31, 1937 issue of the paper. He was on duty in camp one day, and after the enrollees had left for their various job sites, he noticed that "the ambulance which was parked near the dispensary started rolling down the road…picking up greater speed and lo and behold headed straight for the Education Building." Bowens sprang into action and

> *puffed in pursuit of the runaway vehicle. Just as it was about to crash into the building, Bowens jumped on the running board and turned the steering wheel in the opposite direction, thus saving damage to both the building and the ambulance.*

A less heroic but more humorous incident took place two months later on the north shore. The camp writer put it this way for the paper:

The state is going to cover the Chateau [building] with the brightest red paint that can be found on the market. All this is to be done just for the benefit of "Big Moose" Muelver. As big as the Chateau is, he had to run right smack dab into it while he was driving the cat. The reason he explained was that he could not see it and did not know it was there.[76]

Some of the humor found in the paper was a compilation of jokes passed down by enrollees, and some of it was related to true-life incidents. The September 15, 1936 issue of the *Devil's Lake Bluff* reported the following exchange:

About one a.m. the other morning a couple of young strays came back to the fold who had evidently been lost up on the bluff. As they prepared for bed, one of them pulled his G.I. shoe off and slammed it on the floor, waking up everyone around him. He quickly determined he was making too much noise, so he gently put his other shoe down next to his bed. A short time passed when suddenly someone from the other side of the barracks shouted, "Are you ever going to put that other shoe down, so we can get some sleep."

David Rouse remembers that new recruits or younger guys were the most vulnerable to pranks:

I was asked to go fetch a gallon of checkerboard paint from the quartermaster and later to bring back a left-handed monkey wrench. I didn't fall for either ruse, but some of the enrollees accepted the requests at face value.

Most such pranks were not hurtful but could be embarrassing. Rouse remembers, "One night an enrollee came back from Baraboo feeling a little tipsy [and] went right to bed." Four barracks jokesters sprang into action, "each taking a corner, and very gently, very quietly, carried him, cot and all, out to our parade ground, where he was discovered in the morning by our unsympathetic sergeant."[77] The paper didn't report that one, but there were plenty of other personal matters that made it into print.

Enrollees came to expect that any part of their lives was fair game for the gossip column of the paper. Overheard barracks conversations about girlfriends in town, snoring bunkmates and late nights in Baraboo were all fodder for the camp press. But few things could top the typewriter chatter that made Richard "Baby Face" Lessner famous. Being given the nickname "Baby Face" didn't sound much like a compliment, but it was nothing compared to the "Dispensary News" from the March 31, 1937 issue. Lessner "spent six days in the dispensary due to constipation. We'll pray that he does not get that ailment again as he did not take a liking to the method of recuperation." Thankfully, the staff writer didn't go into greater detail.

Aside from Lessner's problem, the paper avoided joking about illness and simply listed those who missed work because of medical

Friendships around camp often began with good-natured pranks and jokes. Many incidents of enrollee horseplay made it into the camp paper, but many did not. *Courtesy Richard McDavitt.*

reasons. Few of those confined to quarters had serious conditions, and many of these conditions involved illnesses not directly related to work. Those included inflamed tonsils, boils on the neck and an enrollee recovering from appendicitis surgery. Camp orderlies watched over the boys, and of course the army doctor assigned to Devil's Lake monitored all cases, keeping strict records as required by district camp inspectors.

Considering the potentially hazardous jobs assigned to the boys, such as rock quarry work, trail maintenance on steep and slippery terrain and building construction, one would expect the camp infirmary to report frequent cases of rock injuries. It is somewhat of a surprise therefore to read the following from the November 15, 1936 paper: "The first aid men are very glad the gooseberry crew is finished for the winter, as most of our sick call in the morning was composed of no one except the men from the well-known blister rust crew."

Even the most diligent watchfulness could not prevent tragic accidents. Grief struck the Devil's Lake CCC community on June 19, 1936. After finishing his workday on the north shore, eighteen-year-old Joseph Poziemski decided to go swimming with a group of enrollee friends. Believed to have experienced intestinal cramps, he disappeared beneath the water fifty feet from the beach. His buddies saw him go under and attempted a rescue, but it was too late. In the six-year history of the camp, his was the only enrollee drowning. The main flag at camp was flown at half-staff in his honor. A one-line tribute in the *Devil's Lake Bluff,* "In Memoriam," was the company's way of saying a final goodbye.[78]

It happened again at Devil's Lake a year after the Poziemski swimming accident. In early October 1937, enrollee John Nosko was killed when he was struck by a passenger train at the north end of the lake. Nosko, age nineteen, was walking the tracks toward Baraboo, on his way to catch a ride to Chicago to visit his mother. Regrettably, the accident was witnessed by a group of CCC boys who were engaged in grading near the tracks. They reported that Nosko appeared to be confused about which set of tracks the train was on, and by the time he figured it out, it was too late. The circumstances appear plausible, yet there is no way of knowing if the young enrollee was perhaps engaging in a bit of daredevil behavior as well. Baraboo officials began a formal investigation, with suicide apparently ruled out. The conclusion was that it was simply a tragic accident. Devil's Lake commander Captain George O'Connor testified at the coroner's inquest and arranged for camp enrollee leader Edwin "Slug" Johnson to accompany the body home.[79]

Editors of the Devil's Lake newspaper occasionally added special features to make the paper more appealing. Every once in a while, the paper added a verse or two of poetry—much of it penned with a message of work, irony and humor. Enrollee Ephriam Wilson got the following printed in the September 15, 1936 edition.

SONG OF THE BLISTER RUST CREW

We're tired, we're mournful
For fate's been untrue.
We're marching along
In the blister rust crew.

We're hot and insulted
When we cease to prance,

The Camp Newspaper

Wilson's right there
With a swat in the pants.

But in spite of all this
At the end of the day,
We always return
Mighty happy and gay.

We'll prove this like nothing
When work is all through
Just notice the smiles
Of the blister rust crew.

Cases of the winter doldrums were also reported in the paper, but the rest of the cold weather news was rarely bad, just lethargic. Winter was a time of partial hibernation, and even leisure opportunities around camp were limited. Confinement and boredom were the worst maladies. It was helpful that the recreation hall had a pool table plus a well-stocked supply of books and newspapers from town. In 1939, the Works Progress Administration (WPA) hired two arts and crafts instructors from Baraboo to begin classes at the camp in the winter. These indoor classes focused on woodcarving, leather craft and beadwork. Woodcarving as a way to pass the time was a long-standing winter tradition among the boys of Company 2669 and is mentioned in several issues of the paper.

Another important part of the *Devil's Lake Bluff* was its periodic welcoming article to new recruits and its send-off to enrollees who reached the end of their enrollment periods and were heading home. For the new people, the message was hopeful and heartfelt, with a reminder that "you have been placed in a camp located amidst scenery that is world famous." Camp rules of conduct were published, plus a final bit of advice on how to treat others living in close quarters: "It is by respect for the other fellow that we ourselves gain respect." It was the job of veteran enrollee leaders like Art McDavitt, Slug Johnson and Big Bob Karow to occasionally back up these printed messages with more forceful discourses in the privacy of the barracks building.

For those departing CCC service, the paper sometimes reserved the front page for an inspiring message from the camp commander, reminding them about the training they had received and how it could be used in the job market. Names and hometown addresses would be listed, along with a final good-luck message from their buddies and the staff of the camp newspaper.

On the day of departure, it was most common for the man who was leaving to sign a few discharge documents in the office and part with handshakes from the commander and a few old friends. Then it was time to catch a ride to the train station. It was a rare treat when someone made a bigger deal of it, but that is what happened in the fall of 1939. The paper mentioned that Devil's Lake commanding officer H.D. Davidson organized a farewell party for twenty-one enrollees. "Mr. Davidson rendered several songs. A lunch of wieners, buns, apples, and marshmallows, followed by the movie *Gunga Din* was provided" before the boys were officially dismissed.

Some of the departed kept in touch with their old bunkmates. In a column titled "Remember Your Mates?" the paper would update the civilian job statuses of those who had gone. For example, the camp paper said that Lon Shay was going to the School of Barbering in St. Paul, Minnesota; Bill Rode found work in a canning factory in Oakland, California; and Willie Bergen got hired at Burgess Battery in Madison. Writing about Devil's Lake veteran Roy Copher, the paper noted, "We have information that Copher would like to be back, and we are sure that he would be made welcome." Such post-service accolades were not always found in many CCC camp newspapers elsewhere in the country.

In the spring of 1937, Elmer Swanson and Earl Belisle drove up to the camp from Milwaukee. They had served a tour at Devil's Lake, been discharged and found employment back home. Now they had come back to visit old friends. It had been a long ride from their hometown, but it was a joyful reunion, with the paper reporting that "both were in high spirits and in spite of being comfortably situated [in their new jobs] expressed regrets of missing the gang."[80]

The farewell issue of October 15, 1941, rightfully paid tribute to Big Bob Karow. The story noted that Bob had been given a medical discharge after being sent to the CCC facility at Fort Sheridan, Illinois. Besides being a sports hero, camp leader and chief cook, Karow was the longest-serving enrollee at Devil's Lake. Starting in 1937, Bob Karow had used his maximum reenlistment options, plus his position as camp leader, to extend his stay at the park. The paper noted that "he has watched a good many boys come and go."

9

FAREWELL

Despite its record of accomplishments, other forces were at work in the late 1930s that changed the outlook for federal relief programs like the CCC. A number of national political decisions, combined with changes in the condition of the American economy, resulted in decreased enrollment in the CCC after 1935. As some elements of the economy began to improve, many young men were able to find work in their hometowns. Thus, enrollment in the CCC and travel away from home became a second or third option for job-seeking teenagers. Reverberations were felt in Washington, D.C. A 1937 debate in Congress to make the CCC a permanent government program stalled and eventually died.

Meanwhile, voices from Wisconsin reiterated concerns about certain aspects of the program. Naturalist Aldo Leopold continued the argument that CCC projects were not properly managed from a conservationist's point of view, doing more harm than good to the landscape they were seeking to improve. Leopold's words carried a lot of weight with wildlife managers and soil scientists but did not resonate with policymakers or politicians at that time. Furthermore, Leopold was immersed in a CCC prairie restoration project at the University of Wisconsin–Madison Arboretum, and his criticism was not directed toward Devil's Lake or any other specific location. In 1938, another voice, Philip LaFollette, son of former senator Robert LaFollette, was pushing the CCC to end the practice of assigning black enrollees from Wisconsin to segregated camps in Illinois.[81] Nothing came from either of these complaints, and neither were Leopold's or LaFollette's viewpoints factors in ending the CCC. The program remained immensely popular with ordinary citizens, who, over the years, could see the benefits the CCC wrought even if their children or relatives had not been enrollees.

Despite the popularity of the program with the public, enrollments continued to decline. The reason was not just the improved job market, for while unemployment rates did fall from their high in 1933, the jobless numbers were still historically dismal throughout the CCC era. Ironically, declining enrollment numbers did make it possible for more local boys still interested in working for the CCC to serve at a camp near their hometowns. In the spring of 1940, almost twenty new recruits from Sauk and next-door Columbia Counties (including recruits Budde and Guetzkow) got assignments at Devil's Lake. While the number of local boys was always small compared to the full complement of two hundred men, the prospect of and convenience of working near home was one way for administrators to encourage future enrollments. Nonetheless, there was a looming problem that had an impact on enrollment, and CCC administrators had no power to control it.

This problem was the war in Europe starting in the fall of 1939. While the United States was not involved at that time, many believed Hitler's march in Western Europe would soon be felt on this side of the Atlantic. The United States wasn't at war, but it was beginning to manufacture military material as if it were. By 1940, war-related products and manufacturing began to turn the economy around. Factories needed more workers, and people began to think differently about their futures. Unemployment numbers were still historically high, but young people could sense that things were changing. Was the CCC necessary anymore? Had young men's enthusiasm for the program disappeared? Also, questions that had come up at the beginning of the CCC were now revisited. Would military drill become a part of CCC camp life? Was the CCC to become a pathway to military service? These questions became more important with each news report of Hitler's conquests and Japanese empire building in the Far East.

Devil's Lake commanders monitored the National Parks camp closings. The news wasn't good. The number of NPS camps nationwide (including state park camps) dropped below two hundred as the decade of the 1930s came to a close. The Badger State, too, had its share of camp closings. As early as the fall of 1937, closures at other Wisconsin state parks left only five parks with CCC units at work. Besides Devil's Lake, the other camps of the lucky five included those at Pattison, Interstate and Rib Mountain State Parks, as well as the University of Wisconsin's Arboretum camp in Madison. It was a small, exclusive club that was about to get smaller.

Dressed for a return to civilian life, two enrollees on their way home stand alongside two barracks leaders for a scrapbook photo taken by enrollee Art McDavitt. *Courtesy Richard McDavitt.*

However, there were projects in the works that Eugene Odbert and other follow-up supervisors could promote as a way of keeping Devil's Lake camp operational. If work projects were in the administrative pipeline, it was likely that those projects would be allowed to finish, and the camp would therefore continue to function. Devil's Lake still had the administration building and other smaller projects into the 1940 season. There was still work to be done in the park as part of the 1941 plan, but by then, all the big stone-building jobs had been completed. Trail work was on the to-do list, but even then, the big trail projects were done or nearly complete. By the fall of 1941, the announcement came, and the curtain finally came down on the CCC at Devil's Lake after six years of remarkable work.

Unfortunately, conditions at the Devil's Lake camp had begun to deteriorate prior to the closing announcement. With the turnover in both enrollees and camp commanders, rules around camp that had been in place since the beginning started to slip. Enrollee Bruce Budde remembers during the 1940– 41 season that it was not necessary to sign out in order to leave camp in the evening. Nor was there a formal time for enrollees to be back in their bunks: "You could just walk out of camp at the end of the day, and if you didn't get back, then you were that much short of sleep." Even though Budde's carpentry duties kept him in camp during the workday, he rarely saw or had contact with the camp commander. All of these things were routine to Bruce Budde in 1941, but that was not the way things had been done when the permanent camp was set up in 1935. The final years did not produce a total breakdown of discipline, however. There was at least one army regulation holdover from the early days. Budde recalls, "We were not dismissed for the weekend till after the Saturday 11:00 a.m. camp inspection. Your footlocker and other barracks had to be in perfect order before they would let you go."[82]

Rigorous weekend inspections notwithstanding, the camp inspectors from the district headquarters began to discover a number of infractions at the camp that weren't present in earlier visits. For example, it was found that bedding and laundry funds had been abused. The camp mess was also experiencing "a great deal of wastage." Clothing and other issue items were not marked "CCC." Nightly bed checks of the enrollees' barracks had been suspended. By itself, each violation was not serious and was easily corrected. Yet the cumulative effect of the charges became a damning statement about camp leadership and how lax standards of discipline on the part of commanders could take an organization down. These infractions gave ammunition to the bureaucrats who were making decisions about camp closings. Times were changing, and world war was on the horizon. The downward spiral of camps closing all over the country had been going on for some time, and it wouldn't take much to justify closing another one.

Camp inspectors at the district level found that many of the problems at camp could be attributed to its leadership command. Experienced disciplinarian commanders like Uitti and Davidson were gone. When he was assigned to Devil's Lake in early 1941, commander William Glasbrenner was forty-five years old and had but four months experience with the CCC. His second in command had two months experience. The part-time doctor was on the job for one month. The inspection report concluded, "It can readily be seen, [the assistant] gives the Commander little help."[83]

Most disturbing to the investigating officer were the discoveries found during a surprise barracks inspection. A number of enrollees were missing. There was a buildup of coal gas due to improper window ventilation, and one enrollee who had been drinking "was found unconscious in the latrine." Needless to say, the inspector forwarded a report noting that the conditions at camp were "entirely unsatisfactory."

Farewell

It was also plain to see why these conditions existed, and Inspector Harold Chafey outlined that in his report. "Camp has just recently had a change of command. Attention is called to the experience of the army administrative personnel: this condition is no doubt due to the current shortage of officers." That fact, combined with fewer enrollments in the program, made for a slippery slope to extinction.

In the meantime, the war in Europe had been an unavoidable topic of barracks conversation late into the night. "We talked about the war and wondered if we would be asked to join the service," recalls Clarence Guetzkow. "I wasn't too anxious to fight, but some of the guys did join the military. Trucks were made available to take them to Fort Sheridan for enlistment." For Clarence and the rest who stayed at camp, there was not much they could do lying in their bunks and thinking about it. The best thing for everybody was to get out and work in the park.

The remaining boys of Company 2669 continued to stay active until the doors were finally closed. In September, they completed work on the East Bluff Trail. Over a dozen men received proficiency certificates for special vocational training in October 1941—the final month of operation. Before they left, the boys recorded one more act of community partnership. The enrollees put down their construction tools for a time and formed a rescue party to find a lost family on the East Bluff.[84]

Young Ted Rozinski was among the group of enrollees who were there when the camp closed. His experience in the CCC is typical of that last group of boys to go through the program. From his parents' farm in Doylestown, Wisconsin, he had been hearing about the CCC throughout his teen years in high school. The local newspaper had been covering its activities and accomplishments for some time. In addition, his older brother, John, had joined and was at Devil's Lake, so young Ted knew exactly what kind of work was going on at the park and heard stories about what life was like at a CCC camp. Wouldn't it be great if Ted could join John there?

The Rozinski family farm in Columbia County was only about forty miles east of the lake. But before Ted could pack his bags and leave, there were some questions to be addressed. Ted's parents, John and Pearl, had a farm to run. One son was already away; could they afford to be without another? A family discussion around the kitchen table ensued. It was the kind of conversation that had been going on ever since the CCC program began. Ted pointed out that if he were to join, two salaries of CCC boys would be coming home. And after all, his brother could probably get him assigned to Company 2669 at the park. He and his brother could then get weekend passes home. The discussion continued until both father and mother relented. With brother John's help, Ted's dream of going to Devil's Lake as a CCC enrollee came true in April 1941. John was one of the assistant leaders among enrollees at the camp, so it is likely that he guided seventeen-year-old Ted (the age requirement had been lowered in 1935) through the first few days. Ted's first assignment was tree planting, and later he helped build stone drinking fountains around the park. But his favorite assignment was truck driving.

Getting behind the wheel gave Ted the opportunity to drive to various places outside the park, picking up and delivering goods and building materials and at the same time conveniently avoiding the heavy lifting of trail work. He was so good at his job that he even drew the assignment of driving the boys into town on the weekends. Shortly before the camp closed, his outstanding driving record earned him a CCC proficiency certificate signed by the camp commander and education advisor.

Only sixty-eight enrollees remained when Company 2669 was disbanded and the camp officially closed on November 1, 1941. For those who had not served out their full enlistments and wanted to stay in the CCC, they were given a choice of which existing camp they wanted to join. Wisconsin camps that accepted Devil's Lake boys included City Point (S-85), Gays Mills (SCS-2) and Pattison or Rib Mountain State Parks.

With the closing of SP-12 at Devil's Lake, Ted Rozinski transferred to Pattison State Park near Superior. While there, he expressed an interest in continuing his service beyond his current enrollment, but war tensions were having an effect on the national program, and he was denied a three-month "reselection." Less than a week after the attack on Pearl Harbor, Ted was formally discharged from the program.[85]

The threat of world war had been an unseen hand slowly pushing the CCC into decline. When the attack came on Pearl Harbor in December 1941, it was as if a hammer had come down on the program. In the face of world war, conservation and park projects suddenly didn't seem important. National defense was the overriding priority now. All camps were ordered closed by the end of 1942 as the United States shifted to a war footing. It seemed like an abrupt end for the enrollees, but their CCC experience was about to pay off for the government. As war mobilization kicked into high gear, it was discovered that training and discipline learned in the camps were useful in the armed services as well. Many CCC veterans used their backgrounds in the "tree army" to boost their standing in the military. Living in the camps taught the CCC boys how to adjust to the army way. It was said that many

World War II army sergeants started as CCC men. World war was certainly a life-changing event for these men, but many would later say that the CCC experience, not their military service, was the most exciting time of their lives.

The directive from the national administrators in Washington said that all camp buildings should be sold, dismantled or moved. Some buildings, because of their portable construction and years of continuous use, were beyond hope and were simply torn down. Even though Devil's Lake fit the profile for standard removal, its location spared it from the wrecking ball. Because the Devil's Lake camp was on state park land, the logical option was to transfer the buildings to the State of Wisconsin. This quirk, plus other special circumstances, saved the camp buildings from instant death.

The Badger Army Ammunitions Plant north of Sauk City and a few miles south of the park was gearing up for the war effort just as the CCC program was winding down. During the war years, the Devil's Lake camp was conveniently used for offices and then employee housing by those working at the plant—extending its government life. After the war, the State of Wisconsin again assumed ownership, but many of the buildings were too run-down to be useful. Some of them were sold to interested individuals, who had them moved out of the park.

By 1975, only four building remained. One of the bigger units was "largely rebuilt" and made available to church groups and others for retreats and meetings. Despite the renovations, the structures nonetheless deteriorated as the years went by. The last two buildings became storage sheds used by the state park staff. In March 1989, a controlled debris fire inadvertently spread to the last remaining building.[86]

The memories of the CCC boys who served at Devil's Lake would of course last much longer than the camp buildings. Enrollee Robert Spees worked at the CCC camp at Pattison State Park just a few miles from his home. He figured the north woods beauty could not be beat, but his three-week, temporary assignment at Devil's Lake opened his eyes to a one-of-a-kind wonder in Wisconsin. He admits that after more than sixty years, it was easy to forget events from his CCC days. However, he still remembers the off-duty walks in the park and going to the Baraboo dances with his new friends at the Devil's Lake camp.[87]

Clarence Guetzkow said, "At the time, I wasn't sure if it did me much good. But as I look back, I now know that it was a good experience." Most enrollees didn't have to wait for the passage of time to understand the lessons learned from their CCC experience. Tom Belken joined Company 2615 in Milwaukee before it was split to form Company 2669 and was with the quarry crew that cut stone for the bathhouse project on the north shore. "I didn't know what it was all about," he said, "but I soon learned. I transferred to Devil's Lake, where I met some of the finest fellows I ever knew. All in all, I had a fine time here and am not sorry for the months I spent in the CCC."

Clarence Van Leeuwen was also with the first group of enrollees to report to Devil's Lake in the summer of 1935. He had his camera with him and took some of the first photographs of the camp. "There were twenty-five of us who established the camp," he recalled. "When the barracks were ready for use, I became company utility man." Clarence also knew why he was there and when it was time to leave. He said at the time: "I like the camp life fine, but I feel that I have been here plenty long, and I have decided to quit and shift for myself."

Bruce Budde was among the last group of enrollees to serve at Devil's Lake but came away with the same lesson the others had learned when they first reported to the park in 1935: "It was a good experience to get away from home and do something on your own. The CCC also taught you how to get along with other people."

Enrollee Al Draws left Devil's Lake in 1936 with a reflection that must have been shared by hundreds of young CCC men who served at the park before and after him. Al saw it as "an invigorating, healthful, interesting experience for any young fellow. It teaches one independence, the ability to shift for yourself, plus order and regulation."[88]

In close quarters, like on the reservoir project, teamwork and understanding one's job were important elements in properly completing the work. *Courtesy Richard McDavitt.*

Farewell

In six years of work, the CCC boys resuscitated the appeal and image of Devil's Lake like nothing else since. When the CCC arrived at the park in 1935, the luxury resorts and excursion boats were gone, but not the tourists. The daily amenities that visitors expected were in short supply, and the state parks system didn't have the financial means to keep up. Without the CCC, buildings would eventually have gone up in the park in response to visitor demand, but it is also certain that actual construction would have been postponed far into the future, certainly lagging well behind visitor expectations.

A remarkable feature of the National Park Service and CCC partnership was how quickly things got done. The wheels of bureaucracy moved incredibly fast for a newly created government agency like the CCC. Credit for swift and efficient camp organization and construction can properly be given to the U.S. Army, but individual projects at state parks were a function of NPS initiative, plus acquiescence on the part of Wisconsin parks officials. Building plans were formed, approved and started within weeks. Yet training, design and construction corners were not cut. Materials were of the best quality available, and job foremen continually inspected all work. Such an outcome was not a foregone conclusion in the beginning.

Proof that the CCC boys changed Devil's Lake State Park is found in just a small sampling of what they did. The stone buildings all over the park are the most noticeable, but there is also the construction of the north shore

Construction of a decorative guardrail along a road leading to cottages on the north shore. *Courtesy Wisconsin DNR, Devil's Lake State Park.*

The finished guardrail. Despite later modifications, the railing is still in place well into the twenty-first century. *Courtesy Wisconsin DNR, Devil's Lake State Park.*

One of the truly unseen projects of the CCC: installing underground telephone lines on the north end of the park. *Courtesy Wisconsin DNR, Devil's Lake State Park.*

parking lot, erosion control for the lake beaches and check dams hidden in the woods of the West Bluff whose silent job it was to prevent hillside erosion and farmland waste from running into the lake. Other big projects involved campground development, including construction of 130 picnic tables. Fifteen drinking fountains were constructed around the park. Thousands of trees were planted, along with restoration and reconstruction of unused roadways in the park. Two temporary bathhouses were built on the south shore, and miles of trail development were initiated throughout the park.

As the supervising unit, the National Park Service fulfilled its mission of incorporating natural design and native materials into parks projects, especially buildings. It handed back to the State of Wisconsin a park that, without NPS planning and CCC participation, would have taken decades to update and modernize. The credit at the top goes to many prominent individuals who used their political clout to get things done. Yet there was no more influential individual at the park during the CCC years than NPS supervisor Eugene Odbert Jr. After five years of service at Devil's Lake, he accepted the position of director of public works at his old hometown of Sturgeon Bay. Then he came back to the Devil's Lake region to serve as public works director for the city of Portage. Odbert was a smart fellow, but it is hard to believe that he would have gotten those public works positions without successfully running the NPS public works projects at Devil's Lake in the 1930s. Enrollee David Rouse, who was among the first group at Devil's Lake in 1935, came back on family vacations to visit his old camps. The camps at Devil's Lake and at his other assignment at Camp Ontario in the western farm country of Wisconsin were, of course, gone. Yet there was something about Devil's Lake that brought it all back. Certainly, the buildings triggered nostalgia, but so did the way the state park service kept the place. The Nature Center helped tell the story of the CCC to visitors, and for Rouse, it "provide[d] an enduring link to pages from my past." Rouse couldn't find that same feeling at his other camp:

> *What a shock we got when we went looking for Camp Ontario! There wasn't even one stick, board or stone left to portray the existence of a once lively encampment. Camp Ontario had reverted back to the farmland from whence it had sprung.*[89]

There were so many things about working in a state park that were different from working at the more numerous national forest or soil conservation camps of the CCC. The biggest difference seemed to be that at the parks,

This view of the completed bathhouse is the last in Eugene Odbert's collection of photographs submitted to National Park Service officials documenting CCC work on the north shore. It was also undoubtedly intended to show how CCC projects could be of immediate use to the public. *Courtesy Wisconsin DNR, Devil's Lake State Park.*

there were always civilians nearby watching what was being done, and what was being done was noticeably undertaken for the convenience of park visitors. Thus, the improvement was often visible and immediately useful to the park tourists. It is a sad fact that most of what the CCC boys did elsewhere across the nation can no longer be seen or is difficult to find. That is not the case at Devil's Lake.

The north shore bathhouse, the biggest CCC building project at the park is still there and serving visitors as a meeting area. For anyone taking a closer look, the state park service has put up a sign identifying the building as a CCC project. Another CCC project still standing on the north shore is the park administration building. Still extant in the Northern Lights campground are the three stone buildings built by the CCC in the late 1930s. Hidden in the drainage area next to the railroad tracks on the north shore are the two stone culverts built by the CCC and still carrying traffic.

The Balanced Rock Trail, winding its way steeply up the talus slope at the south end of the park is little changed since the Depression days. The steps of native quartzite put into place by the young men so long ago have been worn smooth and slick by thousands upon thousands of modern hiking boots. Many of those hikers also use the steps to sit, catch their breaths and admire the view, just as the CCC boys did in 1941. In the old days, the boys

A proud enrollee poses next to his work as a vacationing travel trailer crosses the stone culvert on the road to the Northern Lights campground. Like other stone structures in the park, this one still stands into the twenty-first century. *Courtesy Wisconsin DNR, Devil's Lake State Park.*

A souvenir photo of the camp, circa 1938. Foreman and local experienced man Marven Hartman produced this popular view for sale or perhaps as a gift to enrollees. To many young men without cameras, this photo represented an important, and perhaps the only, reminder of their service. *Courtesy Bruce Budde.*

could look to the southeast from the heights of the trail and see their camp among the pine trees below.

Unfortunately, the Devil's Lake CCC camp, located a short distance from the south shore, is no longer there. Home to about two hundred men during six years of conservation work, the camp's manicured grounds once had nearly fifteen buildings, including a water tower, a garage area for vehicle maintenance and a chapel for quiet reflection. Today, the campsite serves as the large group-camping area for the park.

The group parking area is off South Lake Drive. Turning into the lot, two stone pillars mark the old entrance to the camp. Beyond the parking lot is a cleared grassy area with a modern bathhouse at the other end. A perceptive person standing in the cleared area, or even in the lot, will notice dozens of mature pine trees all around him, some appearing to be lined up in a row. These are the young, five-foot-high pines that the CCC boys saw when they first arrived in 1935. These are the same ones that survived the building construction to serve as landscaping for the camp.

The CCC certainly was good for Devil's Lake State Park, but it was also good for the young men who lived in the barracks and grounds where tall pines now grow. That is what President Roosevelt intended for the program—not just conservation but also maturity and hope for those who would become the greatest generation. When enrollee John Loprieno left the CCC after service at Devil's Lake in 1936, he said:

> *During my year and a half that I have been in the CCC, I think I have had the best experience I ever had. It has taught me how to mix with other people and to make the best of friends; it has taught me how to do any sort of man labor. Now that Chicago is calling me back, I am not afraid to face the outside world, and as the years go by, I'll never forget my fellow friends of the CCC.*[90]

For the young men of Company 2669, duty at Devil's Lake was as much of an adventure as it was a job. It was a chance to make new friends, learn a trade and build confidence and maturity. The boys carried home those memories and skills after their CCC enlistments expired. The bonus for the park is that the area was infused with a huge burst of construction and conservation energy that enhanced visitors' enjoyment while at the same time advancing the science of forest and lake management.

Yet the human element remains at the heart of the CCC. Perhaps no other unexpected, life-changing impact of service can match the

Barracks leader J.E. "Tiny" Brack (left) and "Peanuts" Daulen pose for Art McDavitt's scrapbook snapshot. In the mind of many enrollees, camp friendships were more important than project work. *Courtesy Richard McDavitt.*

experience of Harold Crow. Harold's hometown of Kane, Illinois, was depressingly small, and like so many others, he saw the CCC as a way to shake off the dust of his isolated corner of the state and see the rest of the Midwest as part of a grand and adventuresome tour. Among a group of downstate Illinois boys assigned to Company 2669, Harold was a dark-haired, average-built, eager young teenager of eighteen when he arrived at Devil's Lake camp in 1937.

As for many enrollees, his first view of Devil's Lake was a wondrous surprise. He had no idea how beautiful it would be. There was certainly nothing like this around Kane. Therefore, it didn't matter what kind of work he would be doing; spending time in the park and soaking in the scenery made the various jobs all bearable and even exciting at times. While other men grumbled about the weather, Harold actually liked cold conditions. He even accepted the otherwise shunned experience of night guard in the winter barracks. It was his job to get out of a cold bed on a winter's night (maybe two or three times) and stoke the coal- and wood-burning stoves in the sleeping quarters. It was a lonely yet greatly appreciated duty and the one that would have stuck most in his memory were it not for another.

Weekends were Harold's favorite time in the CCC. He looked forward to getting together with his barracks buddies and going into town to socialize. A select group would ride together in the same vehicle and plan their evening on the way into town. The Saturday trips were as much an adventure as any workday assignment in the woods. Who knows, they might even meet some young ladies. Yet the girl of Harold Crow's dreams would not be found in Baraboo; she would be found as a result of Harold's service in the CCC.

In 1939, Harold left Devil's Lake and got a transfer to the Mount Vernon camp in southern Illinois. Loneliness might have played a part in the decision. The new place was not as beautiful as Devil's Lake, which was always his favorite, but it was closer to home. It was on a weekend pass from camp that he met eighteen-year-old Wilma Stone on a visit to the town of Mount Vernon with his camp buddies. They continued to date whenever he got time off, but Wilma thought she would never see Harold again after he was discharged in late 1940. But love had taken hold, and Harold did not forget about the shy young woman who had first invited him to a friendly card game with other young people from the town. The two of them were married in 1941 and spent the rest of their lives together, until Harold's death in 2007. It was a full and satisfying life, made possible in large part by the CCC. It became an unintended but endearing legacy that, from California to Maine, other CCC boys found love, too, as a result of their service to the nation during the Great Depression.[91]

In 1977, veterans of the CCC formed an organization, the National Association of Civilian Conservation Corps Alumni (NACCCA). Its purpose is to remember the accomplishments and promote the history of the CCC. Its headquarters building in St. Louis, Missouri, includes a small museum and research facility. The members hold a national reunion each year, and each year they lose a few more veterans. They know that one day there will be no more CCC alumni reunions. They have been preparing for that day by continuing to work on two big projects.

Over the years, members have contributed letters, uniforms, photographs and other items of historical significance to the headquarters. From dozens of local chapters around the country come handwritten biographies of adventures in the CCC, diaries of the good times at camp and other oral history records that are found nowhere else. The NACCCA knew that these items would need a home when the organization ceased to exist. In 2005, it donated most of these historical documents to the Smithsonian Institution in Washington, D.C. Properly housed and cataloged, these pieces of history will be available to anyone who wants to step back in time and try to understand what it was like to leave home and work in the woods and farmlands of America. In 2008, the NACCCA merged with the Civilian Conservation Corps Legacy Foundation. The St. Louis museum facility was transferred to the Legacy headquarters in Edinburg, Virginia. The maneuver reflected the diminishing membership of CCC veterans but does not diminish the ongoing efforts of those who are left.

It was the long-standing hope of the NACCCA that someday there would be at least one statue honoring the CCC work in each state where a camp existed. It had no money to pay for such a project. Instead, NACCCA chapter organizations put together fundraisers, state agencies found a little money, local community groups stepped up and even individual CCC veterans came forward to provide help. Once funds had been acquired, placement of the statues became the next most important priority.

In Wisconsin, the determination of enrollee veteran Howard "Howdy" Thompson was chiefly responsible for getting a statue for the Badger State. A consideration for placement was that it should be in a location where people could actually see it. While much of the good work of the CCC in Wisconsin was done in remote areas, the backwoods was not the place to put a statue. It should be placed in an area where CCC work could still be seen, yet in a place that tourists continued to visit—a place like Devil's Lake State Park.

In a shaded area of the large group parking lot on the south shore, just off the pavement, there is now a statue of a young worker and a memorial plaque commemorating the CCC boys who worked and lived here. State park officials have included an informational kiosk at the site as well. At the 2004 dedication, fourteen veterans of CCC service were there to help celebrate Howdy Thompson's dream for Wisconsin. Among the fourteen was Ted Rozinski, the CCC veteran of Devil's Lake who was there in 1941 with his brother when the flag was taken down for the last time.

The story of the CCC at Devil's Lake State Park is one of incredible accomplishment and fading memories. The statue in the group camp, the stone steps on the Balanced Rock Trail and the old stone buildings on the north shore focus attention on the achievements. The day-to-day memories of working in the park remain locked inside the veterans. As those veterans leave us, they leave behind photographs in family albums and faded documents validating their service. They also leave behind stories of adventure, friendships and hard work told to their loved ones. Bits and pieces of those stories viewed through a black-and-white camera, plus brief sentences scrawled on paper, are all we have as a means of understanding what a life-changing time in history it was for them—and us.

NOTES

INTRODUCTION

1. For a brief history of Devil's Lake, see Lange, *Lake Where Spirits Live* and *Ancient Rocks*. Also see Cole, *Baraboo, Dells and Devil's Lake*; and Gruber, *Diamond Anniversary*.
2. Lange, *Lake Where Spirits Live*.
3. Krzeminski interview.
4. *Devil's Lake…Cliff House*.
5. Pradarelli interview.

CHAPTER 1

6. *Devil's Lake Bluff*, September 30, 1936.
7. The impact of farming on the U.S. economy has become less significant since the 1930s considering the fact that by 2000, the percentage of the U.S. population working in agriculture was slightly less than 2 percent. See Dimitri, Effland and Conklin, "20th Century Transformation of U.S. Agriculture." A general cross-section of hardship stories during the 1930s can be found in Shannon, *Great Depression*. A general history of the state of Wisconsin was written during the Great Depression as part of the Federal Writers Project of the Works Progress Administration (see *Guide to the Badger State*).
8. National figures from Alter, *Defining Moment*, 2; Kennedy, *Freedom from Fear*, 160–66. Average wages from McElvaine, *Down and Out*, 17; Glad, *History of Wisconsin*, 356.

9. Representative Amlie's account of conditions in Elkhorn is taken from Uys, *Riding the Rails*, 26. During the New Deal, Amlie was among a small group of liberals who believed Roosevelt was doing too little, rather than too much, to address the conditions of the Great Depression.

10. A full treatment of early New Deal programs can be found in Badger, *FDR*.

11. Rouse, "Pages from My Past," 207.

12. Pradarelli, interview.

13. For general recruitment rules, see *Recruiting Regulations*.

14. Krueger interview.

15. Calkins interview.

16. Paige, *CCC and National Park Service*, ch. 2. The role of the forest service in CCC organization is outlined in Otis, Honey, Hogg and Lakin. *Forest Service*.

17. Nolen, *State Parks for Wisconsin*, 23–30. Nolen's role in the creation of the state park system, including Devil's Lake, can be found in chapter 6 of Tishler, *Door County's Emerald Treasure*.

18. McFetridge, *Appeal for Preservation*. See also *Report of the State Parks Commission*. For a history of the state parks system, see Newton, *Design on the Land*, 555.

19. Ahlgren, *Human Landscape*, 43.

20. Good, *Parks and Recreation Structures*, 5–6. See also Alhgren, *Human Landscape*, 80. For an overview of rustic architecture and the parks, see Tweed, Soullieri and Law, *Rustic Architecture*.

21. *Baraboo Weekly News*, February 14, 1935. See also Wisconsin Conservation Department Series 271. Box 900, folder #1. *Cazenovia Reporter*. Wisconsin Historical Society Archives, Madison.

CHAPTER 2

22. *Devil's Lake Bluff*, October 31, 1936.

23. The problem with well drilling at the new camp was covered as a page-one story by the local newspaper, *Baraboo News-Republic*, on July 6, July 30 and August 5, 1935. See also *Baraboo Weekly News*, August 15, 1935.

24. Mitchell comments from Uys, *Riding the Rails*, 259–60.

25. Guetzkow interview, July 27, 2009.

26. Budde interview.

27. Guetzkow interview, August 24, 2009.

28. Ibid.

29. Huth's medical background is found in Devil's Lake State Park, park history files, vol. 7. Improvements to the dispensary are mentioned in *Devil's Lake Bluff*, November 15, 1936. Rouse's comments are from "Pages from My Past," 210.

30. Guetzkow interview, July 27, 2009.
31. Eugene Odbert, *Narrative Supplementary Report, Monthly Progress Report* (College Park, MD: National Archives Branch Depository, February–March 1936), Records of the CCC, Records Group 79. Winter confinement and disease hit other camps as well, most notably a scarlet fever outbreak at SCS-11 at Mount Horeb, about forty miles south of Devil's Lake.
32. Winkelmeyer's name is found throughout the pages of the camp newspaper *Devil's Lake Bluff* in late 1936 and most of 1937.
33. Heibl is mentioned in *Devil's Mutterings*, February 18, 1938; March 31, 1938. Additional information about Anthony Heibl came from an interview with his son, John A. Heibl, January 24, 31, 2009.
34. Certificates of completion information can be found in *Devil's Lake Bluff*, October 15, 1941.

CHAPTER 3

35. *Work Experience that Counts.*
36. Salmond, *Civilian Conservation Corps*, 139–41.
37. Camp Inspection Reports, Wisconsin SP-12, July 3, 1936. See also Odbert, *Narrative Supplementary Report*, March 31, 1936, 8.
38. *Reedsburg* [Wisconsin] *Times*, November 8, 1935.
39. Kitchen routine comes from Roedell interview, April 17, 2008; January 2, 2009.
40. Lahl interview.
41. *Baraboo News Republic*, April 23, 1940.
42. *Devil's Lake Bluff*, December 30, 1936; February 18, 1938.
43. Ibid., September 15, 1936; December 20, 1936. Guetzkow comments from interview, August 24, 2009.
44. Lahl interview.
45. Rouse, "Pages from My Past," 206.
46. Guetzkow interview, August 24, 2009.
47. Pradarelli interview.

CHAPTER 4

48. A brief historical overview of Baraboo that includes many photographs can be found in Sauk County Historical Society, *Baraboo*.
49. *Baraboo Weekly News*, August 19, 1937.
50. Camp Inspection Reports, Wisconsin SP-12, May 10, 1940, National Archives Branch Depository, College Park, MD; *Baraboo Weekly News*, January 26, 1939. When the camp closed, the local paper estimated that besides the food and material money spent, the CCC annual payroll

of wages and salary for all camp employees amounted to an additional $38,000. See *Baraboo News-Republic*, November 1, 1941.

In early 1939, Devil's Lake camp commander Lieutenant H.D. Davidson paid a portion of enrollee wages in silver dollars in an attempt to gauge how much money was being spent at Baraboo businesses. Businessmen were instructed to "watch for the silver dollars." Apparently, the experiment was a one-time event, and no records exist to identify how many silver dollars made it into the local economy. (*Baraboo Weekly News*, January 26, 1939.)

51. *Baraboo Weekly News*, March 23, 1939.

52. Articles critical of the CCC are few compared to other New Deal programs but can be found in scattered national newsmagazines, especially in the start-up years of the program. In 1938, Devil's Lake commander R.M. Webber assured the enrollees in writing that military drill was not part of the CCC routine (see *Devil's Mutterings*, March 31, 1938). As for elsewhere in Wisconsin, Tishler, in *Door County's Emerald Treasure*, devotes a chapter to opposition to the CCC at that park. In the Peninsula case, it seems the protest was driven as much by political turf battles and the egos of local powerbrokers as it was about the benefits or harm of a CCC camp in the neighborhood.

53. Odbert, *Narrative Supplementary Report*, March 31, 1936, 8. The camp buildings themselves were not design approved by the National Park Service. Because they were constructed using army standards and built as temporary units to be torn down or moved later, they did not use native stone as part of the building process.

54. Guetzkow interview, August 24, 2009.

55. *Devil's Lake Bluff*, March 31, 1937; December 20, 1936. See also *Baraboo Weekly News*, April 8, 1937.

56. *District Spartan*, January 1940. See Also *Baraboo Weekly News*, December 14, 1939.

CHAPTER 5

57. Rouse, "Pages from My Past," 205–16.

CHAPTER 6

58. Odbert, *Narrative Supplementary Report*, March 1936, 1.

59. Ibid., 1, 2. Park popularity figures taken from *Baraboo Weekly News*, January 26, 1939.

60. *Baraboo Weekly News*, May 13, 1941. Camp Madison (SP-14) at the University of Wisconsin Arboretum was a one-of-a-kind CCC camp. Nominally supervised by the National Park Service, the true administrators

were a group of faculty members from the university. The focus of the Madison camp was on prairie restoration, wildlife management and reforestation. G.W. Longenecker was the executive director at the arboretum.

61. Ibid, 10.; Odbert, *Narrative Supplementary Report*. See also *Pictorial Review*, Sparta District, 1939.

62. Blueprint renderings for many Devil's Lake buildings are found in the Wisconsin Bureau of Engineering, Architectural Drawings for Wisconsin Parks in the WPA period. As for the "Ableman District" and the crew sent there to quarry flagstone, the location is now called Rock Springs. There is a direct rail connection from the district to the park that would make it easy to move stone. It is also possible that trucks from camp were used to haul the flagstone from the quarry to the park. Winter conditions are mentioned in Odbert, *Narrative Supplementary Report*, March 1936, 2.

63. *Devil's Lake Bluff*, February 1936.

64. Odbert's comments on weather conditions for 1936 are found in *Narrative Supplementary Report*, March 1936, 1. For summer 1936 weather, see *Wisconsin State Journal*, August 7, 2007. For double-shift schedule, see "Double Shift Speeds Work, Devil's Lake," *Baraboo Weekly News*, June 11, 1936.

65. *Devil's Lake Bluff*, September 15, 1936.

66. Wisconsin Bureau of Engineering, Architectural Drawings for Wisconsin Parks in the WPA period. For a brief overview of architect Bernard Knobla's career, see Schueller, *Rustic Reflections*.

67. Budde interview, August 11, 2009.

68. There is evidence among park history files to suggest that original trail construction on the bluff trails was done by park employees prior to the CCC days. The CCC boys came in and rebuilt the trail to the top of the bluff. However, the "CCC Trail" from the old campsite was newly built by Company 2669. Other trail construction information can be found in the photographic records at Devil's Lake State Park, as well as in the park history files. The completion announcement of the East Bluff Trail is found in *Devil's Lake Bluff*, October 15, 1941.

69. *Devil's Lake Bluff*, October 15, 1941; August 31, 1936.

70. Doll letter; Lahl interview July 9, 2007.

71. Budde interview, July 24, 28, 2009; August 11, 2009.

72. Fire information can be found in *Pictorial Review*, Sparta District, 1939; *Devil's Lake Bluff*, September 15, 1936.

CHAPTER 7

73. Photo evidence and camp information from McDavitt interview, July 23, 28, 2007. For Idaho service, see camp newspaper *Illini*, 1936.

CHAPTER 8

74. Aside from the camp newspapers themselves, the best treatment of the organization and operation of the camp papers is found in Cornebise, *CCC Chronicles*, 24.

75. The full column is found in *Devil's Mutterings*, March 31, 1938.

76. *Devil's Lake Bluff*, May 31, 1937.

77. Rouse, "Pages from My Past," 209–10.

78. *Devil's Lake Bluff*, December 20, 1936. Camp newspaper records are incomplete for the time of the drowning. However, the full story of the incident can be found in *Baraboo News-Republic*, June 19, 20, 25, 1936. Death rates nationally among CCC enrollees can be found in the *Annual Report of the Director of the CCC*. In the June 1941 fiscal report, it was noted that death rates over the life of the CCC had gone steadily down, mostly due to more diligent safety programs at the camps.

79. *Baraboo Weekly News*, October 7, 1937.

80. The enrollee party is mentioned in *Sparta Review*, October 1939. Other quoted information is from *Devil's Lake Bluff*, 1936; *Devil's Mutterings*, 1938. The full collection is located in the library and archive section at the Wisconsin State Historical Society in Madison, Wisconsin. The Swanson and Belishe visit is from *Devil's Lake Bluff*, March 31, 1937.

CHAPTER 9

81. Gard, *History of Wisconsin*, 496–98.

82. Budde interview, August 11, 2009.

83. Camp Inspection Reports, Wisconsin SP-12, February 7, 1941.

84. *Devil's Lake Bluff*, October 15, 1941.

85. Rozinski interview and letter. See also *Devil's Lake Bluff*, October 15, 1941. For camp closing information, see *Baraboo News-Republic*, November 1, 1941.

86. Lange, *Lake Where Spirits Live*, 78. See also Bouche interview, June 13, 2007; Lange interview, June 13, 2007; Devil's Lake State Park history file.

87. Spees interview.

88. Quoted enrollee remembrances are from various *Devil's Lake Bluff* and *Devil's Mutterings* camp newspapers, most from March 31, 1937. The Budde and Guetzkow information is from an August 2009 interview.

89. Rouse, "Pages from My Past," 216. General soil conservation work in Wisconsin and the CCC role in its success are covered in Johnson, *Soil Conservation in Wisconsin*.

90. *Devil's Lake Bluff*, September 30, 1936.

91. Crow interview, August 11, 17, 18, 2007. The shy nature of Wilma Stone Crow was displayed on her first meeting with future husband, Harold. After Wilma and a group of her girlfriends invited the CCC boys to the card game, it was discovered that no playing cards were on hand. Wilma volunteered to go home and bring back a deck of cards. After returning home, she became nervous and uncertain about the upcoming encounter. Instead of returning to the card game herself, she sent her brother to the game with the deck of cards. Harold was understandably disappointed but did not give up his pursuit of the shy and lovely young lady from Mount Vernon.

BIBLIOGRAPHY

BOOKS AND PERIODICALS

Adler, Jonathan. *The Defining Moment: FDR's Hundred Days and the Triumph of Hope*. New York: Simon & Schuster, 2006.

Badger, Anthony J. *FDR: The First Hundred Days*. New York: Hill and Wang, 2008.

Cole, H.E. *Baraboo, Dells and Devil's Lake Region*. 3rd ed. Baraboo, WI: Baraboo News Publishing Co., 1924.

Cornebise, Alfred E. *The CCC Chronicles: Camp Newspapers of the Civilian Conservation Corps, 1933–42*. Jefferson, NC, London: McFarland and Company, 2004.

Devil's Lake…The Cliff House. Undated publicity pamphlet. Wisconsin Historical Society, Madison.

Devil's Lake Guide, Wisconsin State Park. Publicity pamphlet, 1929. Wisconsin Historical Society, Madison.

Federal Security Agency. *Annual Report of the Director of the Civilian Conservation Corps*. Washington, D.C.: U.S. Government Printing Office, 1941.

Federal Writers Project, Works Progress Administration. *Wisconsin. A Guide to the Badger State*. N.p.: Wisconsin Library Association, 1941.

Gard, Paul W. *The History of Wisconsin*. Vol. 5, *War, a New Era and Depression*. Madison: State Historical Society of Wisconsin, 1990.

Good, Alfred H. *Parks and Recreation Structures*. Washington, D.C.: U.S. Department of Interior, National Park Service, 1938.

Gruber, Bonnie. *The Diamond Anniversary: Seventy-five Years of Devil's Lake State Park*. Edited by Kendra Nelson. Madison: Wisconsin Department of Natural Resources, 1986.

Johnson, Leonard C. *Soil Conservation in Wisconsin: Birth to Rebirth*. Madison: Department of Soil Science, University of Wisconsin, 1991.

Kennedy, David M. *Freedom from Fear: The American People in Depression and War, 1929–1945*. New York: Oxford University Press, 1999.

Lange, Kenneth. *Ancient Rocks and Vanished Glaciers: A History of Devil's Lake State Park, Wisconsin*. Stevens Point, WI: Worzalla Publishing Co., 1989.

———. *A Lake Where Spirits Live*. Madison: Wisconsin Department of Natural Resources, 1975.

McElvaine, Robert. *Down and Out in the Great Depression. Letters from the Forgotten Man*. Chapel Hill: University of North Carolina Press, 1983.

McFetridge, William H. *An Appeal for the Preservation of the Devil's Lake Region*. Baraboo, WI: privately printed, 1906.

Newton, Norman T. *Design on the Land: The Development of Landscape Architecture*. Cambridge, MA: Belknap Press, Harvard University Press, 1971.

Nolen, John. *State Parks for Wisconsin*. Madison, WI: State Parks Board, 1909.

Otis, Alison T., William D. Honey, Thomas C. Hogg and Kimberly K. Lakin. *The Forest Service and the Civilian Conservation Corps: 1933–42*. Washington, D.C.: Forest Service, U.S. Department of Agriculture, 1986.

Paige, John C. *The Civilian Conservation Corps and the National Park Service, 1933–1942. An Administrative History*. Washington, D.C.: National Park Service, Department of Interior, 1985. Available online at www.cr.nps.gov/history/online_books/ccc/ccc1a.htm.

Pictorial Review. Co 2669. CCC Sparta District, Wisconsin, 1939.

Recruiting Regulations. CCC Sixth Corps Area, Washington, D.C., 1941.

Report of the State Park Commission to Hon. James O. Davidson, Governor of Wisconsin. N.p., 1907.

Risjord, Norman K. *Wisconsin. The Story of the Badger State*. Black Earth, WI: Trails Books, 1995.

Rouse, David. "Pages from My Past: The Civilian Conservation Corps." *Wisconsin Magazine of History* 71, no. 3 (Spring 1988): 205–16.

Salmond, John A. *The Civilian Conservation Corps, 1933–1942: A New Deal Case Study*. Durham, NC: Duke University Press, 1967.

Sauk County (Wisconsin) Historical Society. *Baraboo*. Images of America Series. Charleston, SC: Arcadia Publishing, 2004.

Schueller, Mary J. *Rustic Reflections of Copper Falls State Park*. Richfield, WI: Rustic Books LLS, 2005.

Shannon, David A., ed. *The Great Depression*. Englewood Cliffs, NJ: Spectrum Book, Prentice-Hall, Inc., 1960.

Tishler, William H. *Door County's Emerald Treasure: A History of Peninsula State Park*. Madison: University of Wisconsin Press, 2006.

Tweed, William C., Laura E. Soullieri and Henry G. Law. *Rustic Architecture, 1916–1942*. National Park Service, Western Regional Office, Division of Cultural Resource Management, February 1977. Available online at www.nps.gov/history/history/online_books/rusticarch/introduction.htm.

Uys, Errol Lincoln. *Riding the Rails: Teenagers on the Move During the Great Depression*. New York: TV Books, 1999.

Work Experience that Counts. CCC pamphlet, 1941. Wisconsin Historical Society, Madison.

UNPUBLISHED MATERIAL

Ahlgren, Carol Ann. "A Human and Landscape Architectural Legacy: The Influence of the Civilian Conservation Corps on Wisconsin State Park Development." Master's thesis, University of Wisconsin–Madison, 1987.

Architectural Blueprints for Devil's Lake State Park, Wisconsin. Wisconsin Historical Society, Madison. Library archives manuscript collection, Wisconsin Conservation Department files. Series 271. Box 900. Madison, WI.

Camp Inspection Reports, Wisconsin SP-12. Records of the CCC, Records Group 35. National Archives Branch Depository, College Park, MD.

Devil's Lake State Park, WI. History file, vol. 7.

Dimitri, Effland and Conklin. "The 20th Century Transformation of U.S. Agriculture and Farm Policy." Electronic Information Bulletin Number 3, June 2005. Department of Agriculture, Economic Research Service. Available online at www.ers.usda.gov/publications/eib3/eib3.htm.

Doll, Pat, daughter-in-law of CCC veteran Walter Lahl. Letter to Robert J. Moore, June 12, 2007.

Narrative Supplementary Reports of the CCC. Record Group 79. National Archives and Records Administration, College Park, MD.

Rozinski, Ted, CCC veteran. Letter to Robert J. Moore, June 28, 2007.

AGENCIES AND INSTITUTIONS

Devil's Lake State Park, WI

National Archives and Records Administration, College Park, MD

National Resource and Conservation Administration, Washington, D.C.

Sauk County Historical Society, Baraboo, WI

University of Wisconsin–Madison

Wisconsin Historical Society, Madison

NEWSPAPERS

Baraboo News-Republic
Baraboo Weekly News
Reedsburg [Wisconsin] *Times*
Wisconsin State Journal

CCC NEWSPAPERS

Devil's Lake Bluff
Devil's Mutterings
District Spartan
Illini

TELEVISION

PBS-TV, American Experience. *Riding the Rails.* Aired April 19, 1998.

INTERVIEWS BY ROBERT J. MOORE

Dave Bouche, naturalist ranger, Devil's Lake State Park, WI. June 13, 27, 2007; July 11, 2007.

Bruce Budde, CCC veteran. Portage, WI. July 24, 28, 2009; August 11, 2009.

Helen (Peterson) Calkins, wife of CCC veteran Hiram Calkins. Sun Prairie, WI. February 2, 22, 2010.

Wilma (Stone) Crow, wife of CCC veteran Harold Crow. Jerseyville, IL. August 11, 17, 2007.

Clarence Guetzkow, CCC veteran. Madison, WI. July 27–28, 2009; August 24, 2009.

John A. Heibl, son of CCC education advisor Anthony Heibl. Sarasota, FL. January 24, 31, 2009.

William Heibl, son of CCC education advisor Anthony Heibl. Cottage Grove, WI. April 20, 2009.

Betty Krueger, daughter of CCC veteran Alfred Krueger. Sauk City, WI. June 13, 2007.

Lois Krzeminski. Chicago resident, wife of author. Verona, WI. January 15, 2009.

Walter Lahl, CCC veteran. Milwaukee, WI. July 9, 2007; April 18, 2009.

Kenneth Lange, former chief naturalist, Devil's Lake State Park, Baraboo, WI. June 13, 2007.

Richard McDavitt, son of CCC veteran Arthur McDavitt. Brentwood, TN. July 28, 2007.

Emil Pradarelli, CCC veteran. Cudahy, WI. June 25, 2007

Louis Roedell, CCC veteran. Mt. Horeb, WI. April 17, 2008.

Robert Spees, CCC veteran. Lake Nebagamon, WI. June 10, 2007.

INDEX

A

Amlie, Thomas (Representative) 22
architectural style "rustic" 30, 31

B

Baraboo, WI 25, 28, 43, 50, 55, 58,
    60, 61, 62, 63, 64, 66, 67, 72,
    74, 120, 123, 131
  CCC commerce 62
  local labor 37, 71
  social connection 66
Bonus Army 33
Budde, Bruce 20, 39, 40, 49, 52,
    53, 56, 58, 97, 104, 126, 127,
    132

C

Calkins, Hiram 25
camp newspaper 21, 38, 57, 72, 93,
    106, 113
  cover 115
  humor 119
  poetry 122
Camp Peone, ID 109, 110
Camp Petenwell, WI (S-51) 32

CCC Handbook 48
certificates of completion 47
  proficiency 129, 130
Chateau 35, 55, 96, 98, 120
Civilian Conservation Corps (CCC)
  African Americans 34
  buildings 40
  camp commander 38, 55, 62
  camp number 26
  company numbers 27
  education advisor 44, 46, 47, 115,
      117, 130
  enrollment 24
  Kitchen Police (KP) 51, 75
  legacy 17
  memorial 141
  military doctor 42
  organization 25
  pay 24
  side camps 32
Civilian Conservation Corps
      Legacy Foundation 141
Company 2669 33, 57, 65, 66, 74,
      129, 138
  accidents 43, 69, 76, 103, 122
  advance crew 36

baseball 56, 118
blister rust crew 101, 121, 122
camp canteen 53
camp closing 130
camp library 44, 52
camp routine 48
enrollee leader 41
field trips 46, 117
fire season 105
fire suppression 105
holiday break 57
inspections 38, 75, 128
living conditions 37
loneliness 74
meals 49
medical emergency 43
open house 69
projects 66, 135
winter 11, 13, 43, 50, 52, 55, 75, 87, 88, 104, 123, 140
Crow, Harold 139, 140

D

Davidson, H.D. (camp commander) 43, 60, 63, 71, 75, 124
Devil's Lake 14, 20
  camping 15
  hiking 97
  Pine Plantation 34
  popularity 15
  railroad 13, 31, 37, 66
  resort destination 16
  side camp 32
Devil's Lake Bluff 115, 119, 122, 123
Devil's Lake State Park
  administration building 95, 96
  Balanced Rock Trail 99, 136, 141
  bathhouse 40, 77, 85, 86, 89, 90, 93, 96, 107, 110, 111, 136
  CCC Trail 99
  East Bluff Trail 100, 129
  Northern Lights campground 94
  park status 29
  side camp 32, 55, 64
Devil's Mutterings 115, 116
Doran, F.M. (camp commander) 35, 62

E

Emergency Conservation Work (ECW) 23, 34

F

Forest Service (USDA) 19, 26, 27, 28, 117

G

Glasbrenner, William (camp commander) 128
Guetzkow, Clarance 20, 39, 41, 43, 52, 53, 58, 59, 60, 67, 99, 126, 129, 131

H

Happy Days 113
Harrington, C.L. 29
Heibl, Anthony J. 46, 47
Huth, Melvin, Dr. 42

J

Johnson, Edwin 57, 118, 122

K

Karow, Bob 52, 57, 111, 118, 124
Knobla, Bernard H. 95, 96
Krueger, Alfred 25
Krzeminski. Lois 15

L

LaFollette, Philip 125
Lahl, Walter 52, 54, 56, 59, 103

Larson, Henry 21
LaValle, WI 51, 57
Leopold, Aldo 125
local experienced men (LEMs) 71,
  85, 90, 91, 98
Longnecker, G.W., Professor 84

M

Macomb, IL 108
McDavitt, Arthur 20, 107
McFetridge, William H. 28
Mitchell, Jim 38

N

National Association of Civilian
  Conservation Corps Alumni
  (NACCCA) 140
National Park Service (NPS) 18, 19,
  27, 28, 80, 81, 93, 133, 135
  camp closings 126, 128
  master plan 85, 100
  structural standards 30
Nolen, John 28, 31
Nosko, John 122

O

Odbert, Eugene 20, 71, 80, 85, 87,
  88, 89, 90, 99, 127, 135

P

Peninsula State Park 64
Poziemski, Joseph 122
Pradarelli, Emil 17, 24, 60

R

Roosevelt, Franklin D. 17, 23, 24,
  33, 44, 47, 71, 112, 138
Rouse, David 20, 24, 43, 54, 73,
  120, 135
Rozinski, Ted 52, 129, 130, 141

S

Soil Conservation Service (SCS)
  19, 27, 108
Spees, Robert 131
Sun Prairie, WI 78

U

Uitti, W.L., Lieutenant (camp
  commander) 69, 70
unemployment 22, 74, 126
U.S. Army 27, 133

V

Van Leeuwen, Clarence 132

W

Winkelmeyer, William R. 46, 47,
  117, 118
Wisconsin
  state parks 19, 29, 126
  state park system 28
Wisconsin State Park Authority 30

About the Author

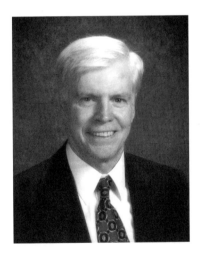

Robert J. Moore is a former high school American history teacher. Prior to his retirement, he was named American History Teacher of the Year by the Arizona chapter of the Daughters of the American Revolution (DAR). Mr. Moore also served for eight seasons as an interpretive specialist for the U.S. Forest Service in Arizona. His duties included research preparation and set up of museum-style displays for the Apache-Sitgreaves National Forests visitors' center. His display on the CCC evolved into his first book, *The Civilian Conservation Corps in Arizona's Rim Country.* His CCC work has also appeared in the *Journal of Arizona History* and the *Wisconsin Magazine of History.*

Since moving to Wisconsin, Mr. Moore has continued to research CCC history with a special focus on Devil's Lake. He has also served as a historical consultant to the Mount Horeb Area Historical Society and Wisconsin Public Television (Madison). He currently lives and teaches in Verona, Wisconsin.

Visit us at
www.historypress.net